WHISTLER

PAINTINGS · DRAWINGS
ETCHINGS & WATERCOLOURS
BY DENYS SUTTON

PHAIDON

SYMPHONY IN WHITE NO. 2: THE LITTLE WHITE GIRL. 1864. London, Tate Gallery

JAMES McNEILL
WHISTLER

PAINTINGS · ETCHINGS
PASTELS & WATERCOLOURS

BY DENYS SUTTON

PHAIDON PRESS

MADE IN GREAT BRITAIN 1966
PRINTED BY HUNT BARNARD & CO LTD · AYLESBURY · BUCKS

JAMES McNEILL WHISTLER

AS AN ARTIST Whistler favoured an approach which was very different from that side of his character he paraded so vehemently in public. There is nothing vulgar about his art, as so often about his behaviour. He was never cantankerous in his painting, in which, on the contrary, he tended to be discreet and even evasive. His pictures with their low-keyed colours are apt to look a little wan and even thin-blooded when compared with many by his contemporaries, a Gauguin or a Van Gogh, for example, and it is only at the present time, after a long and undeserved lapse from public favour, that they have started to attract fresh admirers. His work now scores owing to its possession of qualities which, until recently, have been rather suspect – at any rate, so far as modern art is concerned. The sheer exuberance of so much contemporary painting (in which subtleties of treatment are frequently jettisoned in favour of an immediately effective statement) has occasioned a reaction on the part of some lovers of art; and there is a tendency for these 'reactionaries' to seek refuge in restrained and more evocative painting in which darker and restful tonalities predominate. These can be found with Whistler's work. Yet there must be no misunderstanding. In his own way, Whistler could prove exceedingly daring; indeed, he can exert an important claim on our attention as a precursor of the recent experiments connected with action painting.

Whistler sailed under the banner of 'The Butterfly'. He was volatile and elegant and the sort of man who finds it difficult to settle down. He liked to be on the move. By his own choice he was an expatriate from his native America, where he was born in 1834. However, when settled in Europe, he retained a liking for certain national dishes and proudly boasted of his cadetship at the West Point military academy. Nevertheless, he attached little importance to 'grass roots', nowadays usually considered so necessary and important for a transatlantic artist, and, to use Philip Rahv's striking definition of the American character, he was a 'paleface', not a 'redskin'. He was a true cosmopolitan; so, dispensing with any definite connection with national tradition, whatever that may be, he alighted wherever he came across those oases of beauty which were likely to refresh him. He was essentially an aesthete. This meant that he shared in that dislike for materialism which motivated some of his most gifted and sensitive contemporaries in both the United States and Europe, and, like them, he spurned the crassness and coarseness which disfigured so many aspects of the late-Victorian era. His belief in art was absolute and his approach in many respects was analogous to that of the connoisseur who strives to turn his surroundings into a fastidious barrier against vulgarity and to discover, and make relevant to his own use, those precious qualities in the external world which answer to his own scrupulous love of perfection. It was thoroughly in accord with his attitude that, when looking at the old masters, and he was a keen student of such painters as Canaletto (Fig. 22), Hals, Terborch (Fig. 19) and Velasquez (Fig. 18), he should have derived pleasure, more often than not, from that one passage in a single picture which seemed to enshrine those artistic virtues that appealed to him. The narrowness of his taste arose from the obsessional nature of his vision.

Inevitably, Whistler had to be prepared to pay the penalties arising out of his views. It is the aesthete's disadvantage, and failing even, that he is rarely, if ever, satisfied, and that he is a perfectionist; his is a position which inevitably cuts him off from the warming vigour of life. For an artist, moreover, the wilful pursuit of a conscious aestheticism can prove a dangerous policy; in the end it may engender a certain debility. The very qualities which distinguish Whistler's art – a love of delicacy, an inherent elegance and a delight in a transitory and fragmentary mood – were perilous for a painter like him, who could not summon truly robust artistic resources to his assistance. He could have surrendered more exclusively to the softer and insinuating components in his make-up and given in whole-heartedly to his dandyism; fortunately he did not succumb to this temptation. His very stubbornness and his refusal to compromise provided the sinews for his art and served to support his more delicate fancies; the Puritan, and perhaps the American, in him came to his rescue. Paradoxically, he was saved by another asset and one which, at first sight, might have constituted a weakness. This was the dissatisfaction with his own achievement which may be discerned beneath the carapace of his very complete egotism. The wish to do better and to succeed was central to his character and partly stemmed, it may be suggested, from a sense of inferiority and from his realisation that, as an American, he did not really belong to the European tradition as such. Moreover, he possessed a 'nose' for novelty – another transatlantic characteristic. Such sides to his capricious and lively nature were to activate his creative powers. There is another point as well. The fact that he fell out with many of his friends and pupils, Sickert, for instance, underlines the acute feeling of isolation from which he suffered, and, what is perhaps more important, it throws into relief his confidence in his own mission.

Whistler, at any rate in public, was a very self-sufficient man. Ralph Curtis, a fellow countryman and a fellow cosmopolitan, who knew him in Venice in 1880, summed him up with singular skill: *'Malheur, bonheur,* Whistler conceded nothing – his attitude to art, to himself, to the public, and to his rivals, past and living, never changed. Applauded or booed, he ever remained with the same high aesthetic ideals, and the same shrewd eye to business. A rare combination. To us humble apostles of this faith, the master always seemed an ultra-exclusive aristocrat. In this Gotha of royalties of the profession, picturesquely few did he deign to recognise as "brothers". This ultra-fastidiousness was sincere. It also included, possibly, sentiments of self-defence – a sort of Monroe Doctrine.'

Typically, in delivering his famous and brilliant 'Ten O'Clock' lecture in 1885, Whistler cast himself in the role of the Preacher. With Whistler indeed the Preacher and the Dandy often went hand in hand. However, for many the sparkle of his wit and the preciosity of his turn of phrase, as in this celebrated declaration of faith, frequently obscured the seriousness of his principles and his passionate attachment to them. He was easily misunderstood. But it would be wrong to underestimate the comprehensive nature of his outlook and contribution, abortive though some of his experiments were to prove, and the extent of his drive to revolutionize the contemporary artistic scene. In fact, it is essential to consider as a whole his theories, his admirable and very radical typography, the care he paid to the presentation of his work in specially designed frames and his original manner of staging his exhibitions. He was one of the first artists to insist that works of art should be shown in sympathetic surroundings, and he took great care to arrange a harmonious décor for his one-man exhibitions. He had every ambition to shine as a *homo universalis.* Nothing, under his dispensation, could be left to chance. Although his patron, F. R. Leyland (No. 60), deserves every sympathy for the way in which Whistler treated him, and the caricature of him (Fig. 15) was cruel, he ought perhaps to have realized that his protégé was quite incapable of refraining from providing his own interpretation of the decoration of the dining room of his house, 49 Princes Gate. It was to become the famous Peacock Room now in the Freer Gallery of Art, Washington (Figs. 16, 17).

Whistler was also canny. Thus a constant process of weighing up and testing went on in his mind: rejection is one of the keynotes of his art – he once declared that 'to destroy is to survive'. He was not satisfied with the second best; indeed, the connoisseur's ambition is to find the very best available. This provides the explanation for the endless and painful attempts he made to discover the perfect solution, as he saw it, of any problem he tackled; his words to his close friend Fantin-Latour '*Je gratte tout*' were often only too true.

It was fortunate for him that, when leaving North America as a young man in 1855, he should have gone to Paris rather than London. He was at once in touch there with a determined *avant-garde*. Although he avidly responded to the Realism associated with the modern group then coming to the front in the Paris of the 1850s, reality in the sense that it appealed to a Courbet, a Bonvin or a Ribot could only hold him temporarily. Even in an early and overtly realistic picture such as the *Head of a Peasant Woman* belonging to Glasgow University, or the *Self-Portrait* (No. 1) in the Freer Gallery of Art, Washington, he hinted at the presence of that mysterious inner-world, which resides within us all, and the allusion to which became a major objective of his mature style. Nevertheless, his true personal approach could only have emerged as a result of a contact, at some point, with Realism. It was necessary for him to come to grips with nature in the raw in order to sharpen his appetite for selection and then for synthesis. This contact acted as a vital discipline to him. How incisive in their notation of the outlines of buildings and how responsive to atmosphere, for instance, are the etchings (e.g. No. 4) undertaken on his youthful tour of northern France – the so-called 'French Set' – or those later vignettes (Nos. 5, 10, 14, 16) of river life on the Thames in which he boldly captured the rough features of the sailors and the longshoremen and the stillness of the craft at anchor. It was typical of his alertness to fresh ideas and his sense of the significant trend of the moment that he should have become one of the leaders of the etching revival which occurred in both England and France in the 1850s.

At this stage Whistler was also in the forefront of the painterly revolution; indeed his style, during the 1850s and 1860s, is properly understood only when his rôle as a cross-Channel painter is taken into account. His allegiance, partly to France, partly to England, proved a fruitful alliance. His ties with French artistic circles evidently stimulated his faculties; they made him free of ideas and aims not generally current in this country. *At the Piano* (No. 7) of 1858, in the Cincinnati Museum, is touched with that gentleness of spirit and feeling for intimacy which likewise may be discerned in Fantin-Latour's *Les Deux Soeurs* (St. Louis Museum: Fig. 9), painted in the same year. Yet, when this picture and the *Harmony in Green and Rose: The Music Room* (No. 9) in the Freer Gallery, Washington, are placed in the contemporary context, their individuality and personal quality emerge. These are cuts from life which disclose the artist's delight in suggesting atmosphere by means of a recourse to delicate tonal effects. A comparison between *At the*

Piano and contemporary photographs* also suggests that he was influenced by photography; in fact, the murky backgrounds frequently favoured in his later portraits are comparable to the neutral surroundings used in the portrait-photographs of the time.

Already, too, he had revealed his concern for the spatial arrangement of a composition; this is stressed in a picture such as the *Harmony in Green and Rose: The Music Room;* the positioning of the figures and the interplay of the rectangular shapes of the picture frames are balanced by the mantelpiece. This is a genre picture but without the anecdotic connotations which usually occur in most painting done in his country of adoption at this period. When a certain literary flavour did occur in a picture, as is the case with *The Coast of Brittany* (No. 18) in the Wadsworth Atheneum, Hartford, Connecticut, which was shown at the Royal Academy in 1862 under the title of 'Alone with the Tide', the emphasis was placed not upon a story but upon the mood of a little Breton peasant girl seated on a desolate beach. There is no denying the experimental character of his painting at this phase; and in a picture such as *The Blue Wave, Biarritz* (Hill-Stead Museum, Farmington, Connecticut: No. 19) the use of a breaking wave seems to anticipate one of Coubert's favourite motifs. His close relationship to the modern French movement is brought out in the crisp handling of paint found in the *Wapping*, 1861–1864 (No. 11), in the collection of Mr and Mrs John Hay Whitney, New York. The rendering of the background with its ships and buildings possesses qualities which recall Manet's technique. Incidentally, the connections between the paintings of the two artists, who met in 1861, were rather close at this period and it is just possible that Manet's marines may have exerted some influence on Whistler.

Whistler might easily have become a fully-fledged member of the Paris school. Yet, when faced with the decision of where to settle, he plumped for London. He may have come to the conclusion that he ran more chances of success in this country than in France, where competition was so much stronger; his own words on the subject certainly seem to imply this. The sceptical attitude with which, at a much later date, Degas treated his antics and pretensions makes it clear that he would not have been able to crow so loudly in Paris as over here. He may also have felt, intuitively perhaps, that his particular style could have been stifled in the more ebullient atmosphere of Paris, where, at this point, the emphasis was increasingly placed on energy of expression. Moreover, antipathy to Realism was fundamental to his temperament; as far as his art is concerned, he was rarely seized by that overwhelming passion for life which impels a

*A relevant example is *Three Young Women*, dated to about 1860, which is illustrated in James Laver's *Victorian Vista*, 1954.

painter to involve himself with themes of a richly sensuous nature. An element of fear seems to mark his attitude to flesh painting as if the animal quality of the female form, which is so superbly voluptuous when rendered by a Titian or a Courbet, was too much for him. How unsubstantial, when compared to the pictures of these men, are the *Venus rising from the Sea* of about 1868 (No. 49) in the Freer Gallery, Washington, and the nudes of the 1890s (Nos. 116, 118); and his very abstinence from an enjoyment of the potentialities of this sort of painting may perhaps be interpreted as another reflection of his innate Puritanism, possibly due to his American and Scottish ancestry.

One of the most famous of his early paintings, the *Symphony in White No. 1, The White Girl* (No. 25) in the National Gallery, Washington, was an intimation, had he but known it, of his decision to abandon a realist position. This painting, which won a great success with the Parisian modernists, when shown at the Salon des Refusés in 1863, is a romantic work, not without a neurotic tinge. It is possible to understand the reasons which prompted the art critic Castagnary to interpret this canvas as an allegorical representation of the morning after the wedding night and to compare it to Greuze's *La Cruche Cassée.* Yet the charge of sentimentality is avoided owing to its pictorial values: the light colours, the contrasts between areas of broad paint, the daring of the design and such small, but telling, details as the disposition of the girl's rather untidy hair and the richly treated rug. Courbet's reading of it as an *apparition* was not far wrong and, as such, it possessed that hallucinatory element which grew more dominant in Whistler's art over the years. Indeed, his claim that he was exclusively a 'pure' painter is not altogether borne out by the subject matter of his pictures. Some light on the cast of his mind and of his relationship to the contemporary English movement is afforded by the fact that he should have tackled the theme of the 'White Girl' on several occasions, and that he should have done so was hardly fortuitous. The title itself is surely significant. It may be interpreted as revealing a special attitude; it underlines his sympathy for the idea of virginity, which is discernible in the cult of the 'stunners', then current in mid-Victorian artistic circles. The concept of idolising one's mistress, for 'Jo' was the model for two such canvases, is clearly connected with the romantic imagery of the Pre-Raphaelites.

These artists frequently painted the beloved, who usually had red hair, as a languid and, indeed, rather asexual creature, the very diminution of whose physical appeal made her (at any rate in their eyes) particularly alluring and desirable just because she was remote – an unspotted flower in a rank world.

Fig. 1. Gustave Courbet: 'LE BORD DE LA MER À PALAVAS'. Montpellier, Musée Fabre

Fig. 2. Eduard Manet: THE FOLKESTONE BOAT – BOULOGNE, 1869. Philadelphia, Museum of Art

Fig. 3. Torii Kiyonaga: YOUTH AND COURTESANS. Colour Woodcut. London, British Museum

Figs. 4 and 5. Whistler: STUDIES OF BLUE AND WHITE NANKIN PORCELAIN. London, Julius H. Weitzner

An emphasis on purity, a dash of melancholy and an implicit appeal to masculine protectiveness are apparent in the *Symphony in White No. 2: The Little White Girl* (Frontispiece) in the Tate Gallery, London, and the model's mood is caught by Swinburne's charming verses which were appended to the frame when the picture was shown at the Royal Academy in 1865. In Whistler's case, his transformation of Jo – a healthy Irish girl as she appeared to Courbet – into a dreamy maiden was probably partly conditioned by his own sense of alienation from life.

Though always independent, Whistler was in closer contact with a number of contemporary trends than is sometimes suspected; thus, although deeply revering an artistic tradition, like that of tonal painting, he was not prepared to remain an exclusive heir to the European past; in any event, why should he, as an American, have done so? Like a number of his contemporaries, amongst them Gauguin, he was anxious to broaden his range and to seek nourishment in new and exotic cultures. This desire to strike out and to explore the exotic largely stemmed from the *l'art pour l'art* aesthetic formulated by Théophile Gautier, with whose writings Whistler was almost certainly familiar. This ambition to pursue an escapist route and to avoid conventional limitations was obviously extremely important for his art; above all, it impelled him to reflect carefully on his artistic language and, in doing so, it helped to free him from the decorative sweetness which sometimes threatened to seduce him.

He was one of the first to respond to the craze for Oriental art which captivated many of his friends in Paris and London, amongst them Fantin-Latour and Dante Gabriel Rossetti. He stood out as a pioneer admirer of Blue and White china (see Figs. 4, 5), Japanese woodcuts (Fig. 3) and Oriental screens. These were prizes he avidly sought, and with success. At first, his passion for Far Eastern art* was romantic in character. It is this first approach that accounts for the well known group of 'fancy-dress' pictures, mainly painted in 1864, in which models, draped in kimonos but usually looking rather European in appearance, are set against a background decorated, as was his own home in Chelsea, with fans, prints and Chinese pots. His delight in the charms and elegance of Oriental décor was almost like that of an eighteenth-century artist, but even in one of the most Orientalized compositions, the *Caprice in Purple and Gold No. 2: The Golden Screen* (No. 30), 1864, in the Freer Gallery, Washington, where the chair and the screen are used to diversify and enrich the space, he did not achieve a whole-hearted integration with the

*For a recent study of this topic, see John Sandberg 'Japonisme and Whistler', *The Burlington Magazine* CVI, November 1964, pp. 500–507, and Basil Gray, *The Burlington Magazine* CVII, 1965, p. 324.

principle of Far Eastern design. This influence remained on the surface and, significantly, the treatment of the model's features in one of the first pictures belonging to this group, the *Purple and Rose: The Lange Lijzen of the Six Marks,* 1864 (No. 28) in the John G. Johnson Collection, Philadelphia, suggests his possible awareness of Vermeer. This would be feasible, as at around this date the radical French art critic Thoré-Burger was beginning to spread a knowledge of Vermeer's paintings in modern circles. Whistler would also have known Corot's figure painting.

The Far Eastern influence formed a major component in his style and artistic formation. This cult was, of course, common at the time, especially amongst his French colleagues, including Degas and Manet. Yet the Oriental influence was perhaps of greater moment for Whistler than for any of his contemporaries; it so radically altered his way of thinking and artistic conceptions and released potentialities which were ingrained in his nature. Whistler was an American as well as a European and his absorption in Oriental art and his natural sympathy for its fundamental principles and qualities corresponded to a specific and important strand in the American consciousness. The United States, it ought never to be forgotten, faces the Pacific as well as the Atlantic and the affinities between that country and the Far East are many; in our own century they have made their appearance in the architecture of Frank Lloyd Wright and the paintings of Morris Graves and Mark Tobey. The appreciation of the Far East in Whistler's era was mainly confined to the eastern seaboard, where the traders from Boston and Salem had helped to exploit commerce with Japan since that country had been 'opened up' by Commander Perry, an American naval officer. The passion for Oriental culture, which developed in certain American circles during the latter part of the nineteenth century, was far from being superficial; it answered to definite aspirations: Buddhism, for instance, held a special place in the affections of the Boston Brahmins. It is this connection which largely explains the search for Nirvana that engaged those two sensitive spirits Henry Adams and John La Farge.

Whistler never gave any considered view as to the reasons which attracted him to Far Eastern art and especially to Japanese prints. However, those indefatigable and relentless reporters, Joseph and Elizabeth Pennell, stated that he always spoke of the Japanese theory of drawing. 'His idea,' they said, 'was not to go back to the Japanese as being greater than himself, but to learn what he could from them, to state in his own way and to produce another work of art: a work founded on tradition no less than theirs, and yet as western as theirs was eastern.' Also, he agreed that the definition of Japanese draughtsmanship proposed by one of his satellites, Mortimer Menpes, who had visited this country, corresponded to his own. The connection between Whistler's personal concept of aesthetics and that of the Far East is evident enough: the essence of his approach consisted in a subordination of details to an ideal of harmony and balance – a search not so very different from that incorporated, for instance, in the achievements of Sui or T'ang sculpture. This, of course, should not be taken to mean that such pieces, which were probably unknown to him, exercised any direct influence on his art. It is simply to throw out the suggestion, for what it is worth, that his attitude to art was not so dissimilar from that of the Far Eastern artist. The strong Japanese influence in Whistler's art was pertinent for another reason as well. The Japanese taste forms one of the major components in Art Nouveau so that the affiliations between this style and that of the painter become quite understandable.

Was it a Conradian lure for adventure which induced him to set out for Valparaiso in 1866? Whatever reasons accounted for this mysterious but most important trip, it had one major consequence – he saw the Pacific. The small group of attractive paintings resulting from this journey indicate the change that had begun to take place in his art, above all in his use and choice of colour. The seascapes painted in close proximity to Courbet at Trouville earlier in the same year are primarily exercises in the French master's manner. There is usually an emphasis upon a streaky sky or, as in the delicious *Harmony in Blue and Silver: Trouville* (No. 33) in the Isabella Stewart Gardner Museum, Boston, a tender care for the depiction of the horizon; significantly this approach already manifests a certain predilection for a two-dimensional disposition of space. And he used the paint rapidly so that the creamy pigment imparts a characteristically refined touch to the sails of the ships. On the other hand, in the lovely *Crepuscule in Flesh Colour and Green: Valparaiso* (No. 35) in the Tate Gallery, London, the paint itself has become richer and more harmonious. Yet, although this picture renders an impression of atmosphere and light and, as such, is remarkably precocious in view of the date (1866), the approach adopted was fundamentally different from that of the French Impressionists. These painters sought to analyse the effects of light; in their quest they tried to capture the colouristic values of a particular scene, if need be breaking up the spectrum to do so. Whistler, for his part, had begun to offer a selective vision of nature as a means of communicating his emotional reactions and sensations. He attempted to provide a paraphrase of what appealed to him in a specific scene: thus he was compelled to intervene and heighten the atmosphere, bringing out what he regarded as its essential quality by the use of extraneous and, to some extent, almost symbolical properties like the branches and the Oriental-type signature which occur in the *Symphony in Grey and Green: The Ocean* (No. 36) in the Frick Collection, New York. The apprehension of reality was thus assisted by the use of decorative and evocative features.

'Nature,' he declared in one of the most celebrated passages in the 'Ten O'Clock lecture, 'contains the elements, in colour and form, of all pictures as the keyboard contains the notes of all music. But the artist is born to pick and choose, and group with science those elements, that the result may be beautiful – as the musician gathers his notes, and forms his chords, until he brings forth from chaos glorious harmony.' With this perceptive comparison between painting and music, Whistler immediately involved himself in one of the major artistic debates of the day, one that had been given currency by the German romantics, by Poe and by Baudelaire, and which found a subtle participant in Walter Pater. His interest in this problem revealed his grasp of modern questions. Of particular significance and relevance was his recognition of the artist's determination to employ the picture for the transmission of sensations by means of emotive colours; this, of course, was a practice that was to lead on to the Symbolists and, later, to Kandinsky, Klee and much twentieth-century art.

He was not himself particularly musical (his fondness for playing Negro spirituals on the gramophone irritated Rodin!), but this was of small account. The musical analogy served his purpose; in fact, it served to demonstrate that the artist's principal aim ought to be the establishment of a coherent design built on the harmonious interrelationship of tonalities – not that he was so naïve as to believe (as a luckless critic thought) that the use of one colour should be exclusive of any other. In practical terms, Whistler's adoption of musical nomenclature for his pictures, which he used for the first time in 1867 when the *Symphony in White No. 3* (No. 40) in the Barber Institute of Fine Arts, Birmingham, was shown at the Royal Academy, was designed to proclaim that he would have no truck whatever with the typical Victorian concept of didactic subject painting.

This decision draws attention to the alteration that occurred in his artistic principles in the late 1860s. For it was in 1867 that Whistler turned against *ce damné Réalisme*, as he termed it in a long and revealing letter to Fantin-Latour, and in this, amongst other points, he expressed his regret at not having been a pupil of Ingres. Although at first sight no very real or positive influence from this artist can be detected in his work, the painting of the draperies in Ingres's celebrated *La Source* in the Louvre is rather closer to Whistler's technique than might be suspected. What did appeal to him was the creation of

Fig. 6. Stand at the Paris Exhibition of 1878 decorated by Whistler

EDEN VERSUS WHISTLER

THE BARONET & THE BUTTERFLY

A VALENTINE WITH A VERDICT

BEING

A MOST RARE AND FASCINATING HISTORY, FROM THE PALACE OF THE COURTS, WHEREIN IS SHOWN, WITH MUCH WIT AND CIRCUMSTANCE, HOW THE GENTLE MASTER, UNSUSPECTING, WAS SIGHTED, TRACKED, WAYLAID, CIRCUMVENTED, AND RUN TO EARTH BY COMMERCIAL KNIGHT OF UNTIRING INDUSTRY!

TOGETHER WITH THE AMUSING INTRODUCTION OF THE HIND, HENCHMAN, EXPERT AND GO-BETWEEN.

AND, FURTHER ON, SETTING FORTH THE METHODS, DEVICES, CAJOLERIES EMPLOYED FOR THE ENSNARING, ENTRAPPING, BEWILDERING, AND FINAL

Fig. 7. Title-page for the book 'The Baronet and the Butterfly' designed by Whistler

Fig. 8. The Whistler Memorial Exhibition held in London at the New Gallery, Regent Street in 1905

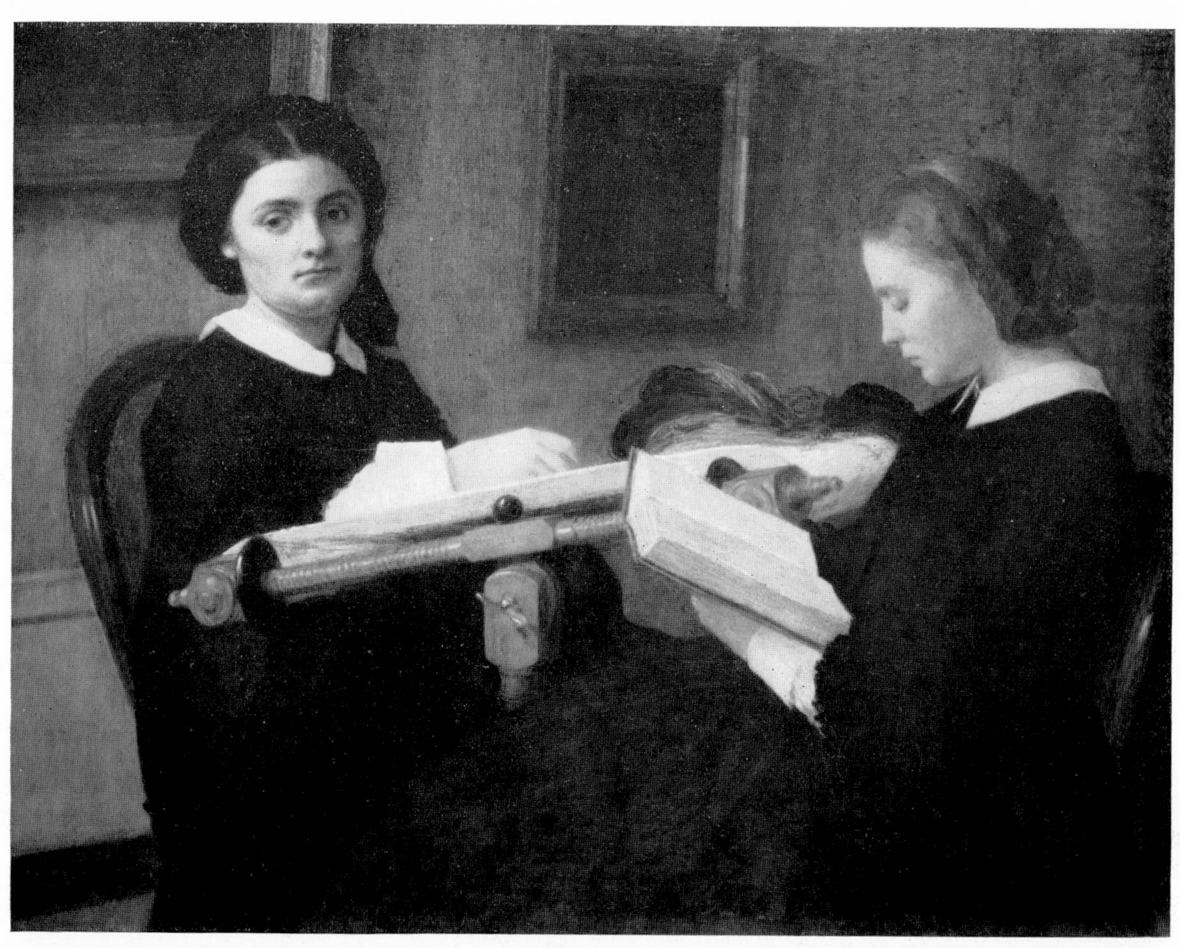

Fig. 9. Henri Fantin-Latour: THE TWO SISTERS. 1859. St. Louis, City Art Museum

Fig. 10. Henri Fantin-Latour: 'HOMMAGE À DELACROIX'. Paris, Louvre

Fig. 11. Toulouse-Lautrec: PORTRAIT OF PAUL LECLERCQ. 1897. Paris, Louvre

Fig. 12. Edgar Degas: THE BELLELLI FAMILY. 1859. Paris, Louvre

Fig. 13. TERRACOTTA STATUETTE FROM TANAGRA. About 300 B.C. London, British Museum

Fig. 14. Lord Leighton: STUDY FOR THE 'DAPHNEPHORIA'. Chalk drawing. London, Victoria and Albert Museum

some sort of link with the idealistic tradition, which, in the several and different ways pursued, for example, by Puvis de Chavannes and Hans von Marées, intrigued painters in the second half of last century. (Some of his drawings are very closely related to those of Puvis or Lord Leighton, Fig. 14.) With Whistler, this trend also prompted a return to the past.

It was characteristic of his cultivated eclecticism that his love for the Far East should have been complemented by an interest in Antiquity. His classicism was never full-blooded and he did not soak himself in the Antique like Puvis de Chavannes or Leighton; nor was he attracted by the formalistic qualities of Greek sculpture in the 6th and 5th centuries B.C. His choice of early sources was typical of the man in the sense that he fastened only on that specific sort of art which accorded with his own aspirations – the sweeter and more decadent sides of Hellenism, to which he was partly introduced through his friendship with Albert Moore, an artist whose work he deeply appreciated. Whistler was a keen admirer of those Hellenistic terracotta statuettes which, after the discovery of Tanagra in the 1870s, were just then coming into fashion; they were available in the Louvre or the British Museum, while the collection of his friend and patron Alexander Ionides was especially rich in pieces from Smyrna. It is obvious that the poses of many of the women in his oils, pastels and drawings were derived from such prototypes (of which he owned an album of photographs) and even in some of his most typical and, for their time, modern portraits like the *Arrangement in Black and Brown: Rosa Corder* (No. 71) the eternal inspiration of Greek art can be sensed. His eclectic spirit was revealed in the series of enchanting and vivacious oil sketches in the Freer Gallery, Washington – the *Six Projects* (two of which are reproduced, Nos. 42, 43), where the Greek and Japanese strains are blended so as to produce a sort of latter-day Hellenised Orientalism. The *Six Projects* also indicate his skill and delicacy as a sketcher in oil. Their technique, which could conceivably owe something to Delacroix's, though the pigment is never quite so impasted as with this master, is extremely individual. It is very direct and spontaneous in effect. The colours are placed on the surface, which is board, with boldly executed streaks, and this treatment endows the paint itself with a crispness and succulence which, in fact, had been noticeable in Whistler's pictures almost from the very start; such qualities may be observed in the *Thames in Ice* (No. 13) in the Freer Gallery, Washington, which was exhibited at the Royal Academy in 1862. It is this considered respect for paint as such and an understanding of its potentially magical properties which were to come out in the later Nocturnes.

Whistler's ambition to create a series of large-scale compositions was frustrated. He had not as yet found the right direction; for instance, he had intended to paint a big canvas in which the artist himself, his models and his friends, Fantin-Latour and Albert Moore, were to be depicted in his studio, and the idea for which may have been prompted by Courbet's *Atelier* (now in the Louvre) or Fantin-Latour's *Le Toast* (1865), which the painter subsequently cut up*. It was a picture, Whistler told Fantin, that would express all those things which would shock the Academicians. Yet it never materialized; in the end, all that resulted were the two very charming and delicate oil sketches now in the Art Institute of Chicago (No. 45) and the Municipal Gallery at Dublin respectively. After painting the *Variations in Flesh-Colour and Green: The Balcony* (No. 44), in the Freer Gallery, Washington, he intended to execute a life-size version of it for the Paris Salon; this was never painted, although a sketch in the Birnie Philip Bequest, Glasgow, may have been connected with its evolution. Moreover, the project for a *Symphony in White No. 4* did not eventuate, but the two oil versions in the Freer Gallery, Washington and the Tate Gallery (No. 41) illustrate his ideas for it. Fortunately, as it turned out, Whistler gave up such essays at this juncture, returning to a closer study of the world around him. Now, however, in contrast to his earlier paintings in which nature was the direct inspiration, his observations and findings were enriched and tempered by the artistic experiences he had undergone. He was no longer concerned with Realism in the ordinary sense, but with the attempt to pass beyond its frontiers and to enter a new world. It was his very personal version of idealism. He accomplished this not by looking back at the Antique world, which had no sustained meaning for him, but by seeking out the spirit and the significance of certain aspects of the night in a great city, London; and the result was the creation of a virtually new genre – the Nocturne.

The title 'Nocturne' was not coined by Whistler himself, although its musical associations are clearly connected with his use of the word 'symphony'. At first, he called such nocturnal paintings 'moonlights' and the term 'Nocturne' was proposed for them by Leyland and, as Whistler wrote to him, 'it does so poetically say all I want to say and no more than I wish.' What Whistler had in mind was confirmed by a further statement made apropos one of his most mysterious and evocative night pieces, *Nocturne in Grey and Gold: Chelsea Snow* (No. 80) in the Fogg Art Museum, Cambridge, Mass., in which he declared: 'I care nothing for the past, present or future of the black figure, placed there

*The portrait of Whistler from this composition is now in the Freer Gallery, Washington.

because the black was wanted on that spot. All that I know is that my combination of grey and gold is the basis of the picture. Now this is precisely what my friends cannot grasp.' His object in such pictures, as almost invariably in his work, was to achieve a decorative solution for the problem set and, in doing so, he propounded a new and highly poetical formula. Although some of his earlier canvases of the Thames had been painted after nature, this was not the case with the Nocturnes. He would make rough drawings of a motif while boating on the Thames at night or out walking – quick sketches which captured the essence of the scene. Next day these would serve him as the basis for a painting. In other words, following on the teaching of Lecocq de Boisbaudran, with which he had been familiar since his Parisian period, though never that painter's pupil, he worked from memory, staking all on a combination of selectivity and synthesis.

The clue to such pictures is their simplicity; nothing is out of place. The economy of his method was underlined by the fact that he chose to paint night scenes in which colour was restricted to a muted range. He was after the tonal impact of the scene. In keeping with this preoccupation was his contention that, when the night was grey, the sky was likewise grey and the water too; therefore the picture itself must be painted on a grey ground and only once was a white one employed. In fact, the ground of a Nocturne was selected in the same way as a paper for pastel; it was selected so as to accord with the prevailing tone of the picture he had in mind or with a colour that would give him that tone, not so as to avoid work, but 'to save disturbing and embarrassing the canvas'. Whistler's Nocturnes are by no means monotonous, and several convey an extraordinary sense of excitement. The peaceful dreamy atmosphere of the Thames bathed in a faint mist which was evoked in some pictures was counterbalanced by others in which he revealed a willingness to take risks. The exploratory side of his art is nowhere better seen than in the two famous pictures *Nocturne in Black and Gold: The Falling Rocket* (No. 70) in the Detroit Institute of Arts, and the *Nocturne in Black and Gold: The Firewheel* (No. 67) in the Tate Gallery, London, which were both inspired by the fireworks in Cremorne Gardens, the celebrated pleasure resort. They are astonishingly daring works in which, as Ruskin correctly observed, 'a pot of paint' is flung in the public's face, but not, as he claimed, out of Cockney impudence but in order to secure unusual and striking effects – colouristic effects expressive of a particular sensation.

Whistler's technical experiments stress his determination to find means, novel and painterly ones, corresponding to his intentions. For the mid-twentieth century, they may be said to enjoy a special relevance in so far as they indicate the extent to which he was a precursor of the method known as 'drip' painting. In fact, he used a 'sauce' composed of different tones in the dominant colour of the picture. This 'sauce', which he mixed before beginning work, was sometimes employed so liberally that the picture had to be laid on the floor in order to prevent it from running off; and, thereafter, the paintings were frequently placed in the sun to dry. This radical way of treating the picture surface was displayed in at least two of the pictures he painted of Cremorne Gardens before it was closed down in 1877. For instance, in the *Cremorne Gardens No. 3* (No. 81) in the Freer Gallery, Washington, the illusion of a brightly lit portico is secured by shrouding the left portion of the canvas in darkness; and, oblivious to any demands of 'finish' (the gravamen of the charge levelled against him by Ruskin and others), he allowed the 'sauce' to flow freely over the lighted portion of the canvas. No less dramatic in its almost total refusal to move outside a restricted colour range is the painting *Nocturne in Green and Gold: Cremorne Gardens, London, No. 4* in The Metropolitan Museum of Art, New York, in which only a few sparse areas are illuminated: the figures themselves are indicated by means of summary dabs of pigment. The Nocturnes admirably reveal Whistler's considerable skill, especially as the scope of this genre brought into play his particular gifts. In a number of earlier canvases, like the *Nocturne in Blue and Green: Chelsea,* 1871 (No. 65), belonging to Miss J. Alexander, London, the actual handling of the paint, which although rather sketchy is incisive none the less, recalls that found in *The Thames in Ice* (No. 13) in the Freer Gallery, Washington, or the *Harmony in Grey: Chelsea in Ice,* 1864 (Private Collection, London, No. 34). He continued in his Nocturnes that atmospheric treatment of the river and its background which can be already noticed in *The Last of Old Westminster,* 1862 (No. 22) in the Museum of Fine Arts, Boston. In the Nocturnes, the brush strokes impart a dynamism to the surface, establishing, as it were, almost instantaneous marks on the canvas, and the connection with the visible scene is still retained. However, in several of the later Nocturnes – the *Nocturne* (No. 79) in the John G. Johnson Collection, Philadelphia, is a particularly beautiful example – a film of atmospheric suggestiveness envelops the composition, with the result that the beholder is transported into a poetical world in which time and space no longer matter in literal terms.

What counts with such pictures is not the accurate description of the scene but its presentation with strictly pictorial means – colours and signs on the canvas – and these are more significant and indicative of the lasting reality of a

Fig. 15. Whistler: THE GOLD SCAB. 1879. San Francisco, Mrs. A. B. Spreckels

Figs. 16 and 17. HARMONY IN BLUE AND GOLD: THE PEACOCK ROOM designed by Whistler, 1876–77

moment of vision than any precise reproduction of the same site and moment could hope to be. Such pictures point to Whistler's kinship, despite the difference in the methods employed, with an artist such as Gauguin, for had not that great adventurer written: 'In painting one must search rather for suggestion than description, as in music.' Such works provide a novel conception of space in which blues, greens, greys and blacks co-exist harmoniously and thereby create a delicately adjusted tonal equilibrium: here and there the incisive contrasting stroke of colour supplied by a gas lamp contributes a certain weight to the pattern established. His independence of the past was shown in his virtual abandonment of the rules of classical perspective. His study of the Japanese woodcut, for instance, enabled him to conceive his pictures as a flat surface: moreover, his appreciation of Canaletto (Fig. 22), an artist he greatly admired, and the Dutch seventeenth-century school helped him to paint a broad expanse of water in one unified tone. These are works that create an illusion of silence and suspense: the mysteries of night are revealed and endowed with a special and enthralling poetry. He enhanced the magic and familiar scene in such a way that since his day we have never again been able to see the Thames at nightfall without recalling his interpretation:

> And when the evening mist clothes the riverside with poetry as with a veil and the poor buildings loose themselves in the dim sky, and the tall chimneys become campanili, and the warehouses are palaces in the night, and the whole city hangs in the heavens, and fairy land is before us – and the wayfarer hastens home: the working man and the cultured one, the wise man and the one of pleasure ceases to understand, as they have never ceased to see and Nature, who, for once, has sung in tune, sings her exquisite song to the artist alone, her son and her master – her son in that he loves her, her master in that he knows her.

These famous words from the 'Ten O'Clock' lecture are those of a true Romantic. Although Whistler disclaimed any wish to convey a literary mood – his pictures, in effect, are essentially visual – his choice of dusk or night accorded with certain definite contemporary preoccupations. It was a choice that reflected something of the Romantic's constant reaction against the increasing garishness of the modern scene. It was an approach, also, that brings to mind the consolations afforded by night, as when Dante Gabriel Rossetti, tortured by recriminations and a prey to melancholy, wandered through the London streets on his nocturnal excursions. This moment of nightfall, *l'heure bleue,* which appealed so deeply to Whistler, is one when dreams and regrets are engendered: reveries envelop the mind; and passions, too, as Baudelaire had disclosed in *Les Fleurs du Mal.* It was hardly surprising that various writers of Whistler's generation – Wilde, W. E. Henley and Arthur Symons for instance – found inspiration in his interpretation of what, to them, was a congenial and meaningful subject-matter, or that Seurat should have sympathised with his love of painting nocturnal scenes.

Whistler once told the Pennells that 'the painter must also make of the wall upon which his work is hung, the room containing it, the whole house, a Harmony, a Symphony, an Arrangement, as perfect as the picture or print which becomes part of it.' Almost from the very start, his paintings reveal his delight in decorative values, and this is evident, for instance, in the careful way in which curtains are draped to the best advantage or picture frames and dados related one to another in his canvases. There was never anything casual about such arrangements. His concern for decoration is fundamental to an understanding of his art. Thus it is understandable that he became one of the leaders of the reaction against the muddled and eclectic principles of interior design which had been embalmed in the Great Exhibition of 1851. Not for him the crowded interior so typical of the Victorian era; he believed in plain walls distempered in simple colours. Thus he naturally turned to Oriental art for his inspiration and derived support for his ideas from it: his use of yellow must surely be traced back to the Japanese print.

Unfortunately, his typical decorative schemes have not survived; the famous Peacock Room, originally in Leyland's London house and now in the Freer Gallery, Washington (Figs. 16, 17), is an exception to his general principles. This room, which provoked a notorious story by no means to the artist's credit, is one of the most individual decorative ensembles executed in England; and, as an example of exotic design, it is comparable to the Prince Regent's Pavilion at Brighton. The appeal of the room would probably have been greater if the artist himself had been responsible for the original design; as it turned out, the low-hanging pendants, the innumerable shelves designed to accommodate Leyland's collection of Blue and White, and the proportions themselves create a rather enclosed and oppressive atmosphere. As such, it is contrary to Whistler's ideas on interior decoration with their emphasis on simplicity. Only with the gorgeous peacocks, painted in blue on the gold shutters, did his feeling materialise for a bold and telling design. This makes a most effective decoration and indicates that Whistler had presumably derived some inspiration from Oriental screens. This connection is specially underlined in the little known sketch of peacocks, now in the Birnie Philip Bequest at Glasgow. Historically, too, his designs for this room are of some importance as they anticipate certain sides of Art Nouveau: the peacocks themselves with their elegant, curvilinear appearance are sketched in with a sweeping movement which points ahead to a façade like that for Endell's Elvira atelier of 1897 in Vienna, which is so typical of this style. This stylistic relationship was also brought out in the rather unpleasant caricature of Leyland – *The Gold Scab* (Fig. 15) in Mrs A. B. Spreckels' collection at San Francisco. Whistler's forward-looking role as a designer was likewise emphasised in the Primrose Room with which he collaborated with J. W. Godwin for the 1878 Paris exhibition (Fig. 6).

His interest in decoration and in the Nocturne hardly suggests that portrait painting as such appealed to Whistler and that he strove so hard to succeed in this department and to overcome his various limitations. For a start, as he chose to restrict his colours to an almost monochromatic scheme, his finesse in matching shades and tones was continually called into play. Moreover, he was reluctant to build up a portrait slowly in the sense that each section had to be painted in turn; on the contrary, in order to obtain the effect desired, which was really the apprehension of that mysterious quality in any personality which reveals the individual, he had to provide, as it were, an instantaneous statement of the special spark which vivified this inner world. He had to catch that moment when all the elements which held his attention and revealed this essence fused simultaneously in front of his eyes so that he could perceive and render their true meaning – at any rate, in his view. He sought, in fact, just that one pose or that one expression on a face which, to him, spelled a confession.

The evolution of Whistler's style as a portrait painter is singularly intriguing. It indicates that, in the attempt to track down the operations of his mysterious inner spirit, he pursued a course of continuous refinement. It was a pursuit that, in the long run, almost compelled him to abandon the task; the problems he encountered were so grave and the demands he made on himself so taxing that he wavered. And what is also unusual about his portrait painting is that, in a way which is rather similar to the inception of the Nocturnes (and many of these were painted concurrently with the portraits), he hit upon that style, which he made so much his own, almost from the beginning. The *Arrangement in Grey and Black No. 1: The Artist's Mother* (No. 53) in the Louvre, for instance, is an indubitable masterpiece and one of his earliest portraits. It is a very direct and even intense painting which is built up by means of the rectangular lines constituted by the picture frames and dado which serve to set in relief the austere features of Mrs Whistler, restrained and dignified, seen almost as in a cameo. The rather monumental character of her pose, which later influenced

Toulouse-Lautrec when he painted his *Portrait of Paul Leclercq,* in the Louvre (Fig. 11), made one contemporary critic wonder if the artist had seen the statue of Agrippina in the Capitoline Museum at Rome or Canova's statue of Napoleon's mother at Chatsworth. The mood of repose found in this picture parallels that apparent in Degas's *Portrait of the Bellelli Family* (Fig. 12) of 1859 in the Louvre, and both would seem to belong to that moment of 'classical' calm that occurred in French painting just before the revolutionary explosion of Impressionism.

Whistler's liking and flair for modernity are rarely in doubt. Yet in developing his portrait painting, he made a deliberate decision to model himself upon certain earlier artists. He was indebted to Frans Hals and Terborch. His love for both these men is well known; indeed, there is a moving account of Whistler, not long before the end, intensely studying Hals's pictures in the Museum at Haarlem. It is a scene that calls to mind Proust's account of Bergotte's death before Vermeer's *View of Delft* in the Dutch exhibition at the Jeu de Paume. It is Hals's example that may explain the rather broader handling of paint observable in some of his later portraits; and Hals, it ought perhaps to be recalled, was especially influential on American late-nineteenth-century portrait painting.

Yet it was Velasquez who most deeply and truly inspired Whistler. He had grown to love and respect this master shortly after his arrival in Paris, and this at a time when the Spanish painter was also admired by Manet and the *avant-garde*. Significantly, Whistler travelled to Manchester to see the Old Masters exhibition in 1855, which contained a number of pictures by, or attributed to, him, and he copied the *Thirteen Cavaliers* in the Louvre (Fig. 20), then attributed to Velasquez, but actually by Mazo. It was perhaps characteristic of Whistler's ambition that he should have turned to such an inscrutable painter. From him he derived sustenance for his love of tonal painting. An echo of the Spanish artist's silvery qualities may be observed, to take but two examples, in the curtains in the *Arrangement in Grey and Black No. 1: The Artist's Mother* (No. 53) in the Louvre, and in the dress worn by Lady Meux in the dazzling and very modish portrait of her in the Frick collection, New York (No. 91). It was from Velasquez again that he took the conception of a tall figure, lurking in the shadows; and even towards the end in the late *Gold and Brown: Self Portrait* (No. 124) of about 1898 in the Birnie Philip Gift, Glasgow, he remembered his hero: in this instance, the composition appears to be based on *Pablo de Valladolid* (Fig. 18) in the Prado, a photograph of which belonged to Whistler.

Fig. 18. Velasquez: PABLO DE VALLADOLID. Mid 1630's. Madrid, Prado

Fig. 19. Terborch: PORTRAIT OF A YOUNG MAN. London, National Gallery

Fig. 20. Mazo: THIRTEEN CAVALIERS. Paris, Louvre

Fig. 21. Vermeer: THE LITTLE STREET. Amsterdam, Rijksmuseum

Fig. 22. Canaletto: VENICE – UPPER REACHES OF THE GRAND CANAL WITH S. SIMEONE PICCOLO. London, National Gallery

Fig. 23. Whistler: UPRIGHT VENICE. Etching. 1880

Fig. 24. Whistler: PORTRAIT OF AXENFELD. Etching. 1860

Fig. 25. Whistler: PORTRAIT OF SWINBURNE. Etching

A study of Velasquez doubtless encouraged the development of that side of his art which demands that forms and colours be arranged to accord with an inner harmony. 'Techniques in painting,' declared R. A. M. Stevenson, in his book on Velasquez (1895) published in Whistler's lifetime, 'must be understood as a method of using any medium of expression so as to bring out a character or a decorative pattern, or to convey the sentiment with which you regard the appearance of the external world.' This technique, he maintained, was impressionistic; and in his view, and Whistler's too, this had nothing whatever to do with the dissolution of light and the use of pure colour, as practised by the French Impressionists: its essence lay in the subservience of every part of the picture to the whole – to the total effect. This was Whistler's method.

A further connection between the art of Whistler and that of Velasquez may be discerned in the fact that both painters felt a natural sympathy for those passages in a portrait which when seen in isolation could be considered as still life. Spendid details of this sort are to be found in the portraits of Cicely Alexander and Rosa Corder (Nos. 56, 71); however, the emphasis upon a detail of this type was not so strong that it, in any way, disturbed the relationship with the general tonal uniformity. Passages of still life may also be found in such compositions as the *Symphony in White No. 4* (No. 63) and in the decorations Whistler executed for the Peacock Room (Figs. 16, 17).

The acuteness of wit which marked Whistler's conversation was, in a sense, paralleled by his acumen in finding the pose of a sitter he wanted. He perceived the attitude that summed up the personality in a flash. And he knew how to present the pose in a way that rendered the character: think only of the *Arrangement in Grey and Black No. 2: Thomas Carlyle* (No. 57) in the Glasgow Art Gallery and Museum. This is a variant on that used for the portrait of his mother, but how admirably it serves to bring out the sitter's temperament, his melancholy and ill health! Or, how the warmth and self-confidence of the virtuoso are suggested in the no less celebrated *Arrangement in Black: Pablo de Sarasate* (No. 95) in the Carnegie Institute, Pittsburgh: the violinist is seen as an isolated figure, viewed from a distance at a moment of hushed expectancy. For all his proud statements as to his exclusive concern with pictorial values, Whistler, when he wanted to, could render character with decided insight. This skill in defining personality stressed his understanding of human beings and without it he would not have turned to portrait painting at all. This quality marks a number of his etchings, especially those of Axenfeld (Fig. 24) and Swinburne (Fig. 25); that of the latter succeeds in hinting at the more curious sides of the poet's temperament.

The majority of Whistler's male portraits – those of Leyland (No. 60), Irving (No. 76), Duret (No. 92), Sarasate (No. 95), Montesquiou (No. 121) and Vanderbilt (No. 123), to mention only some of the most famous – are traditional full-lengths and with them, as with Velasquez or Van Dyck, the distance between the sitter and the spectator is accentuated. No familiarity is asked for, none accepted, in such pictures. Despite their similarity in stance they are not typed portraits in the sense that they may be felt to have been turned out from the same mould; each is given individual treatment, within the range set by the artist, and correspondingly in each the personality is allowed to appear with delicacy and perception. Once seen, his portraits are not easily forgotten; they remain as characters as well as pictures. He makes us aware that his sitters believe in their individuality and that they are proud, determined men. In a way, moreover, when looking at his portraits and thinking of his own personality, it is tempting to suggest that, by a sort of sympathy, he imparted something of his own dandyism to many of them. They are men of his world as well as of the world. Such portraits suggest that Whistler, however unconsciously, subscribed to the programme laid down by Baudelaire in the Salon of 1840: 'the true painter we are looking for, the one who can snatch the epic quality from the life of today and can make us see and understand, with brush and with pencil, how great and poetic we are in our cravats and our patent leather boots.' These are portraits which are never gay and effervescent as are those painted by the Impressionists; on the contrary, they represent the inhabitants of a shadowy inward country.

The distinction, which marks the best of his portraits, partly arose from the care with which they were prepared. He would frequently and, of course, quite legitimately stack the cards in his favour before beginning work; thus the daylight had to be adjusted and the colours prepared in advance. Fortunately, some idea of the way in which he set about portrait painting may be gained from Théodore Duret's recollections. According to this writer, who sat to Whistler, the artist, having placed him against a loose grey material, started the portrait without the assistance of any preliminary drawing, slightly marking with chalk the place for the figure on the bare canvas, and, at the end of the first sitting, the scheme was already present, with the colours and tones it was to possess in its definitive state. At this point, the artist's determination to achieve perfection became evident; and after the picture had been brought almost to completion, it was rubbed out; work was begun all over again and finally repainted some ten times, over a considerable period. Whistler's conviction that strong personal intervention was necessary is also revealed in one of his most exquisite and adorable early portraits – the *Harmony in Grey and Green: Miss Cicely Alexander* (No. 56) in the Tate Gallery, London. For this picture he selected the muslin for her dress and posed her on a special carpet of black and white tape. The result is a gentle poem in honour of the charms of youth in which the tonalities, the crisp paint, the butterfly hovering over her head, the dado which stabilises the composition and her expression, tender yet determined, present a picture not unworthy to be placed besides a Velasquez.

Feminine beauty brought out the best in Whistler and he became one of the most elegant and accomplished portrait painters of women in the late nineteenth century. His gallery of charmers are of such varied types; the austere Mrs Huth, belonging to Lord Cowdray, the romantic Mrs Leyland (No. 61), the fashionable Lady Meux (No. 91), the spirited Lady Archibald Campbell (No. 93), Jo (No. 25) and Maud (No. 62), and the adorable Mrs Whistler herself, his beloved Trixie (No. 96). To be made free of their company is something of a privilege, and his was the skill to evoke a considerable range of feminine moods; this is proved by the contrast afforded between Mrs Leyland and Lady Meux: the one still belongs to the romantic world of the Pre-Raphaelites, the other is an ornament of a fashionable set. It is his sense for the *mot juste* which renders Whistler's portrait paintings so acute and delectable. The very pose given to Lady Archibald Campbell in the well known portrait (No. 93) in the Philadelphia Museum of Art is a case in point. She is seen standing in left profile, with her head slightly turned towards the spectator and burrowing behind her furs: the pose seems absolutely appropriate and hers by right, even if in fact she was not too pleased with it. What he suggests, rather subtly, is her adoption of a well bred unconventionality within the framework of her status in society; after all she was more than a shade daring in her personal conduct. And what of the brilliant *Arrangement in Black and White No. 1: The Young American* (No. 62) in the Freer Gallery, Washington? With her self-assurance, her desire to get on and her belief in feminine equality (which can surely be read into the portrait), the girl (who is Maud) could step out of the pages of Henry James: presumably 'Miss Gunton of Poughkeepsie' resembled this resolute young person! But Whistler could also obtrude a claw; and is one being unfair to claim that his portraits of his formidable sister-in-law Miss Rosalind Birnie Philip at Glasgow University bring out the vinegary qualities that can also reside in the feminine spirit?

Part of Whistler's success in the major portraits lay in his solicitude for relating the figures to their background and in arranging just that setting which suited them. For that he had a very shrewd eye. He understood that feminine allure is assisted by the appropriate clothes and setting. Thus, in the *Symphony in Flesh Colour and Pink: Mrs Leyland* (No. 61) in the Frick Collection, New York, the introduction of sprays of almond blossom and the use of dotted and patterned matting, together with the rose-tinted wall, with its low dado, serve to endow the composition with a charming decorative appeal. His arrangement of the properties in this particular picture is intriguing for another reason: it seems to anticipate some of the effects found in the portraits of the Austrian painter Gustav Klimt (Fig. 26). This relationship once again underlines his connections with the Art Nouveau movement. The sparse backgrounds of his pictures, moreover, herald the *amor vacui* of some of the English Art Nouveau designers.

Whistler never achieved the popular success he hoped for as a portrait painter and his declared ambition, after his return to London from Venice, to paint 'all the fashionables' did not materialize. That he failed to win general support and acclaim was understandable; his scrupulousness as an artist meant that he was incapable of hurrying with a portrait and, for their part, his sitters were rarely able to afford the time he demanded. Moreover, he could be infernally cheeky, as Lady Meux discovered to her indignation, and, as a consequence, Whistler lost a considerable patron. Nevertheless, towards the end of his life, several important commissions came his way, notably from compatriots, amongst them George Vanderbilt (No. 123); however, by this stage, Whistler's desire for perfection was so intense that he rarely succeeded in finishing off a picture.

It may well be that Whistler had the misfortune to achieve the style he wanted, and which suited him, too early on. He employed this to advantage, yet he was condemned to refine away at a method which he had already established, and which was not susceptible of any marked development. There are variations from the pattern: these are obvious. But what failed to come to his aid at the phase when his style had been pushed almost to the limit was an exuberant sense of adventure and a boldness of invention. These virtues would have proved helpful once an approach had been exploited and well nigh exhausted; they would have permitted him to renew himself by turning in other, and perhaps less explored, directions. Perhaps he was born at an inappropriate moment – that is to win through completely as a portrait painter. He no longer lived in an epoch when painter and sitter were both anxious to secure a rendering of the likeness in similar terms. His sitters, or at any rate the majority of them, wanted their public likenesses, but Whistler had other aims in mind; he preferred to give that special quirk which revealed their personalities, and by no

Fig. 26. Gustav Klimt: PORTRAIT OF ADELE BLOCH-BAUER. Vienna, Oesterreichische Galerie

Fig. 27. Whistler: PORTRAIT OF MALLARMÉ. Lithograph

means everyone was prepared to accept this interpretation. He made his position very clear. He was determined to use his sitters as the excuse for a composition a Harmony, – a Symphony, an Arrangement – conceived in strictly pictorial terms. That the likeness, such as it was, happened to occur was more of an afterthought; not that, on the whole, he failed to catch the right note. Yet, a statement he made in the latter part of his life is highly revealing: 'As the light fades and as the shadows deepen all petty and exacting details vanish, everything trivial disappears, and I see things as they are in great strong masses; the buttons are lost, but the sitter remains, the garment is lost, but the sitter remains; the sitter is lost, but the shadow remains. And that night cannot efface from the painter's imagination.'

Whistler's connection with the French Symbolist movement was of prime importance; it may be seen, as much as anything else, in his love of twilight, and it is particularly interesting to find that Debussy so greatly admired his work, and the composer's nocturnes may have owed something to those of the painter. Whistler's affinities with French art are nowhere better seen than in his close intimacy with Mallarmé – '*mon Mallarmé*' as he called him. They had really met for the first time in about 1886–1887 and remained friends until the poet's death in 1898. The exchange of letters between the two men* which ran from 1888 to 1898 attests the sympathy which bound them. What could be more touching than Whistler's words to Mallarmé after the death of Mrs Whistler: '*Je suis enfin toujours seul – seul comme a du l'être Edgar Poe à qui vous m'avez trouvé d'une certaine ressemblance – Mais en vous quittant, il me semble dire Adieu à un autre moi! – seul dans votre Art comme je le suis dans le mien – et en vous serrant la main ce soir j'ai éprouvé le besoin de vous dire combien je me suis attiré vers vous – combien je suis sensible à toutes les intimités de pensée que vous m'avez témoigné.*' It was singularly appropriate that Whistler should have made such a delicate and telling lithograph of his friend (Fig. 27), one which distills the elegance and refinement of his character and art.

The men had much in common. They shared a mutual liking for delicate craftsmanship and delighted in the impeccable presentation of their works. Also, it is possible to detect some affinities between Mallarmé's fondness for alliteration in his poetry and Whistler's devotion to tonal painting. And both went in for an allusive intimation of the objective world. 'To designate a thing directly,' wrote Mallarmé, 'is to suppress three-quarters of the poem's value which consists in gradually gaining an intimation of the depths. To allude, to suggest, therein lies the dream.' In his own way, this is what Whistler attempted

*See *Mallarmé Whistler Correspondance*, edited by C. P. Barbier, 1964.

to do in his later portraits. These are mysterious and withdrawn, and, more often than not, the essential quality of the personality is stamped with a tinge of sadness. Thus there is present, in a discreet and secretive manner, a reflection of the pessimism which overcame the *fin de siècle*. Yet the difficulties, given the means to hand, of actually intimating such elusive characteristics were very real. They may well explain why it was that he rejoiced in operating on a small scale, as in the portrait of Lucas (No. 98), *Rose and Brown: The Philosopher, Charles Edward Holloway* in the collection of the Comte de Ganay, Paris, or *Mrs Charles Whibley Reading* (No. 114) in the Birnie Philip Bequest, Glasgow.

Whistler's affection for the cabinet picture accorded with his admiration for the Dutch seventeenth-century school; and his later paintings, from the point of view of subject and size, may be related to those of such French Intimists as Bonnard or Vuillard. Nevertheless, the differences between their work and his are significant; for one thing, he did not on the whole adopt a radical colour scheme, stemming from the experiments of Gauguin and the Pont-Aven school or the dynamic colouring of Degas. He nearly always remained faithful to sobriety in his tonal painting. However, like those of these French painters, his small pictures reflect a close and delicate attention to nuances of meaning and colour. This aspect of his art is happily shown in the many oil studies, which date from immediately after his stay in Venice in 1880, and, on the whole, they have been unjustly neglected. It was in this city that he discovered an approach that suited him perfectly – the small sketch in a variety of media. In his sketches he aimed at noting down a transitory effect of light or of movement. Such works spared him the undeniable hardships which were his fate when he attempted to finish a more ambitious project; with the sketches, he was required to do no more than rely on his own sensibility. The stimulus afforded him by Venice was astonishing; there he produced not only the series of wonderful etchings but innumerable pastels.

In Venice Whistler could be himself; there he was away from the competitive and irritating London whirl. There were available simple and unaffected subjects which thrilled him; his is a secret Venice like Henry James's. We are shown the familiar sites – the Riva or the Salute – but also we are introduced to the unexpected. He loved the small half-forgotten *calli* and the archways through which he could peer into tumble-down, picturesque courtyards and note, without any hint of patronage, the appearance of the gondoliers, the bead-stringers and the poor of Venice as they lived their existence, impervious to the stares of the tourist. He takes us into gardens, romantic and off the beaten track, the perfect setting for some impassioned and circumscribed encounter, or shows us a smithy, thus striking a note of realism, almost unexpected in the dreamlike surroundings of Venice, and then a view of the Palaces (No. 88) wrapped in the soft sheen of night and as puzzling and inspiring as anything in Poe. All this is captured in the Venetian etchings; and their quality is superlative. Unlike his paintings, which were worked at in the studio from memory or from notes, the etchings were drawn directly on the plates (a small store of which he would carry about with him), though he did not scorn topographical exactitude. They were revolutionary for their date, as, in them, the contours were not indicated but suggested; it might even be claimed that his etchings, with their hints, their broken lines and their unfinished touches had a true impressionistic quality. It is tempting to believe that Whistler may have studied the drawings of Guardi in which just this quality may be found.

Affinities with Guardi are also to be found in Whistler's Venetian paintings, and there is a strange and doubtless quite fortuitous connection between the effect made by this artist's fragment *Gondola on a Lagoon* in the Poldi-Pezzoli Museum, Milan, and the *Nocturne in Blue and Silver: The Lagoon, Venice* (No. 84). Like his Venetian predecessor, Whistler captured the romantic mood of the city and it may have been due to his desire to do no more than evoke the fugitive impressions to be gleaned that he painted so little while there. For all that, he remains one of the most poetical and original interpreters of the city, and the degree of his sensitivity can be gauged when his work is compared with that of Sargent.

The innumerable small oils Whistler painted in the second part of his life are wonderfully alert; they are charged with intensity. These minute delicious studies, almost invariably painted on panel, are composed with little more than a few dashes of paint in which the tone is perfectly captured and preserved. They are just right. His use of tonalities goes back to Corot and, like this artist, he delighted in greys, greens and ochres. They are unpretentious and direct pictures which translate a sensation into pictorial terms. Such are the melodious harmony and fitness of proportion and colour that mark the best of them that they, rather than his grander compositions, effectively carry out his ambition to impart musical qualities to painting. Their spontaneous quality is striking: so is their discipline. 'It was,' as Sickert* very neatly observed, 'the admirable preliminary order in his mind, the perfect peace in which his art was with itself, that enabled him to aim at and bring down quarry which, to anyone else, would have seemed intangible and altogether elusive.' The elusive quality

*For a recent account of Whistler's relations with Sickert see Andrew Dempsey 'Whistler and Sickert: A Friendship and its End'. *Apollo*, LXXXIII, January 1966, pp. 30-37.

is present all right, but not at the expense of painterly values. It is quite fascinating to see the way in which so briefly and deliberately he stated his intentions: the way, for instance, he could establish the order which marks a building by means of a judicious intermingling of linear rhythms and warmly-hued tones, purplish and brownish, as in the painting *A Shop with a Balcony* in the Birnie Philip Gift, Glasgow. (Such pictures, although luminosity was not his aim, surely indicate that he had looked at Vermeer's *Little Street* in the Rijksmuseum, Amsterdam, a photograph of which he owned.) The lightness and freshness of his sketches are such that they could display a brilliant and whimsical sense of movement so that in the delicate yet dynamic *Chelsea Shops* (No. 103) in the Freer Gallery, Washington, the figures almost possess the enchantment of ballet dancers.

These are pictures in which Mallarméan allusiveness is displayed. Whistler appears to hint at inner meanings and to provide the stuff for interpretation; thus, a strange hallucinatory atmosphere is suggested by the presence of the two old women in *Gold and Orange: The Neighbours* (No. 101) in the Freer Gallery, Washington. Although it is his way of handling paint that counts above all, at the same time it is possible to wonder if he wished to convey a meaning in some of his oil studies. As Whistler was ever deliberate in what he did, it may be assumed that the choice of title was not arbitrary. In a study like *The Sad Sea: Dieppe* in the Freer Gallery, Washington, the spatial disposition brings out the content; the two-dimensional planning, the anonymous figures, the economy of treatment, the enclosed atmosphere, the sense that everything has a limitation but that the sea is ever present, all this is hardly fortuitous: it is the expression, in gentle tones and in a restrained manner, of a state of mind – a sad one.

The sympathy for the intimist approach and for the relationships that bind human nature which occurs in a number of the oil studies may likewise be found in many of his lithographs: particularly relevant and charming are the *Jardin du Luxembourg* (No. 107) and *The Duet* (No. 113). He was a talented lithographer who also used this medium for nocturnal scenes, and in his prints of Vitré, colours were employed. Yet it was typical of his independence that he did not really share in the technical experiments of the Parisian *avant-garde* at this time; for instance, he did not draw the conclusion from Japanese woodcuts in the way that Toulouse-Lautrec did in his graphic work.

Whistler's lithographs of Paris are not as well known as they deserve to be, and in them – as in his small oil studies – he depicted the life of the *quartier* with considerable charm and skill. As in his Venetian pastels, he succeeded in

Paris, in suggesting the less familiar sides of the city; he was after the little note which illuminates a mood or a place. His images remain, so that even today the wanderer who saunters down the Rue du Bac or finds his way to the Rue Furstemberg may well see his surroundings with an eye conditioned by Whistler's art.

Although as a young man Whistler had been in close touch with many of the French *avant-garde* who admired him greatly, this was not quite the case in later years. Whistler himself was apt to be derogatory about some of the major men of the time. Nevertheless, his art achieved something of a vogue in France of the '90s. His *Mother* (No. 53) was acquired for the French nation in 1891 after a campaign led by writers such as Mallarmé, Gustave Geffroy and Duret, and this picture exerted some influence on Toulouse-Lautrec, while Seurat sympathised with his Nocturnes. Yet it was with men of letters that he had the greatest success, and in a sense it was paradoxical that a painter who so strove to avoid literary overtones in his art should have done so.

Mallarmé was not alone in his affection for Whistler as man and artist. Robert de Montesquiou, that 'Prince 1900', as Philippe Jullian has termed him, became a devotee and disciple. Indeed, Whistler's dandyism was largely instrumental in stimulating the cult of aestheticism which occurred in Paris at this time and had one of its high priests in Montesquiou. It would seem as if Henry James had introduced the Comte Robert to Whistler in 1884. Subsequently they became firm friends, and in 1891 he sat to Whistler for his portrait (No. 121). This was finished only in 1894, in which year it was shown at the Salon. It would appear that this was only so owing to Montesquiou's insistence. In a letter to Montesquiou, Whistler declared:

'*Que vous avez raison cher poète. Que j'etais fou. Il est splendide, un vrai d'Artagnan, je ne me pardonnerai jamais mon indigne modestie et crainte, mais quelle inspiration d'avoir envoyé le chercher et juste à temps, car est venu un ultimatum du Champs-de-Mars, il est donc parti le Chevalier Noir.*'

The letters exchanged between the two men during the 1890s, indicate that they were linked by their mutual attachment not only to a belief in art for art's sake but to the principle of mystery in art. Montesquiou in one of his many letters to Whistler whom he would address as '*Cher diable angélique*', wrote: '*Le mystère dans toutes ses formes étant, je pense bien, la chose du monde avec laquelle je suis dans les meilleurs termes et qui, loin de m'épouvanter, me séduit le plus*'.

It is also significant that Proust was fond of Whistler's painting. Although they met on only one occasion, when the writer took away with him the painter's glove, which he had forgotten, as a souvenir, he wrote about his art with singular understanding in his novel *A La Recherche du Temps perdu*. Whistler also contributed something to the character of Elstir in this novel. Proust hung a reproduction of Whistler's portrait of Carlyle '*au pardessus serpentin comme la robe de sa Mère*' in his bedroom and even struggled out to see the memorial exhibition of 1905, telling Marie Nordlinger: '*L'autre jour, bravant la mort (et hélas! la trouvant presque) à l'heure où je me couche, rompu, j'ai pris à la place un fiacre et suis allé voir les Whistler. Ce sont de ces choses qu'on ne ferait pas pour un vivant.*' It is quite clear that Whistler's art was very well known in Paris and it would be interesting to discover what the Intimists – a Bonnard or a Vuillard – thought about it. Whistler himself would certainly have seen the early work of both these painters which was included in the two exhibitions of the International Society of Sculptors, Painters and Gravers held in London in 1898 and 1899. Others represented were Monet, Manet, Sisley and Toulouse-Lautrec.

The oil studies, the Nocturnes and the famous portraits constitute Whistler's achievement as a painter. However, the final phase in his career is of considerable fascination; then he tried, perhaps fruitlessly, to make what can only be termed a fresh start. His letters to his wife reveal that, in 1895, he underwent a sort of crisis, but that, at the end, he felt that the problems facing him had been surmounted and, as he said, 'ease comes where was toil, and all is simple and clear where once was vexation and doubt'. What actually took place in Whistler's mind at this juncture is by no means clear; nor are matters made any easier by the allusive, and rather highfalutin, tone of the language employed in these letters. Yet it does seem as if the artist himself considered that he had experienced a freshening of impulse. A rather more direct note, for instance, can be discerned in the *Little Rose of Lyme Regis* (No. 112) in the Museum of Fine Arts, Boston, or the sombre *The Little Forge, Lyme Regis* at Glasgow University. It was as if Whistler was intent on trying to discover a new connection with his subject matter, and he was clearly seeking to find new formulae. Not that all his ventures were successful; for instance, a picture like the *Phryne the Superb* (No. 115) in the Freer Gallery, Washington, which he himself greatly admired, stand out as little more than a ghostlike reminiscence of the 1860s and as an echo of his abortive idealism of that period. He was more successful in the many delightful pastel drawings of the same model that date from this time. It was at such a moment that Whistler shows himself in the role of 'The Butterfly', hovering on the brink of a new departure but not quite able, all the same, to break the conventions. He did not have the gift of an Odilon Redon who was able to conjure up fresh moods from paint and to invoke the creatures of the secret and subterranean world of impulse and passion; Whistler drew back from this world – and the moment passed away. Although the general tenor of his work was restrained, Whistler painted a number of watercolours which are extremely radiant in tone, and of these certain of the views of Amsterdam and the little known *Interior at Thoresby*, which almost has a Turneresque quality, are amongst the most striking and effective.

There is something extremely sad about the final years when, after his wife's premature death from cancer, he wandered from place to place until his own death in 1903. It was not, however, that he abandoned work. He founded an art school in Paris and engaged in various other projects, amongst them the presidency of the International Society of Sculptors, Painters and Gravers in London, which did much to spread a knowledge of contemporary foreign art in England. He continued to paint – portraits such as the realist studies of Carmen and small oil studies of the sea. But much of his energy was reserved for painting young girls, and the series of oil sketches that resulted are often highly attractive. Stylistically they suggest that he had looked at Carrière as well as Hals and Velasquez; some even recall French eighteenth-century art. At their best, they are direct and fresh and in them he expressed a variety of moods. Pathos was not excluded from such pictures as the *Lillie* in the Birnie Philip Gift, Glasgow, and one of his final pictures, *Dorothy Seaton — A Daughter of Eve* (No. 127), in the Birnie Philip Gift, Glasgow, is touched with a feminine sensuality, the intimation of its presence, rather, and this was hardly discernible in his earlier works.

It is by no means easy to know how such studies ought to be interpreted. It seems evident enough that he had always been attracted by adolescence: this is made clear by his many pastels and drawings of slim girls, and, characteristically, he appreciated Degas's sculpture of the Dancer in her tutu. Can any significance be attached to this taste? Through the ages the artist has frequently drawn inspiration from youth, for one reason or another. In this respect it is perhaps just worth recalling that Henri de Régnier in his fictional portrait of Whistler as 'Cyrille Buttelet' in *La Peur de l'Amour* (1907) hinted at this character's taste for young girls. It would obviously be wrong to try to read too much into an interpretation of Whistler's character in these terms, and in any assessment of his nature and his art it is necessary to guard against too knowing (and Freudian) a view. Yet, at the same time, it has to be remembered that in the nineteenth century many men were fascinated by the image of the pure little girl who can be groomed for marriage and then turned into an ideal partner: the point was brought out by Henry James in his daring early novel *Watch and Ward,* written some twenty years before Whistler painted this particular group of studies, and put into practice by a contemporary artist Frederick Sandys, who married a child-wife. Whistler surely hinted at this sort of concept in his depiction of Jo – in real life the very opposite of a dreamy virgin – in *The White Girl.*

'You have done too much of the exquisite not to have earned more despair than anything else,' Henry James once wrote to Whistler. He was right. Whistler was a master of the exquisite, gifted with an extraordinarily light touch. Yet his art was deeper and more fertile than is sometimes admitted. His sense of space for one thing was exceedingly subtle and in the mysterious Nocturnes he created a silent art in which shadows and masses take on a deep personal significance, not without its poignancy. His also was the ability to take us into the painter's own private world of brush strokes where dimly seen backgrounds are enlivened with rich movements of paint and warm tonalities. This passion for tonal relationships and for a perfection of harmony and equilibrium answered, and corresponded to, his needs as a painter and as a Man as well. They reflected perhaps the obsessions of a personality with many inner tensions; thus he could only secure relaxation when he bathed, as it were, in the repose conveyed by such pictures. It is this sense of a determined desire to express his emotions that gives to his art the intensity which Ezra Pound rightly found in it. Pessimism and frustration tinge his art and yet delight is present; above all his is an art which is marked by awareness. It was part of his achievement that his painting anticipated certain modern movements such as abstraction and drip-painting. Yet in the end what really counts is the personal magic which is conveyed in the variety of media he employed; this was a magic that resulted from the artist's immediacy of response and from his grasp of the particularity of each single experience. This magic emerged simply because the notation of the definite in the obvious sense was discarded and the inner essence of art and life (as it appeared to him) was allowed to float very subtly and fragrantly to the top.

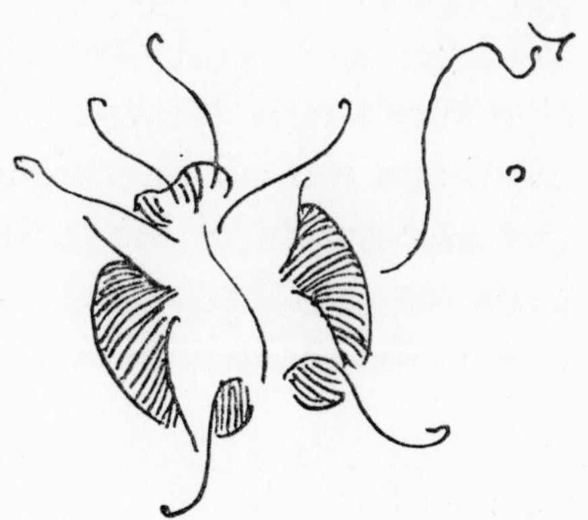

THE TEN O'CLOCK LECTURE
TWO PROPOSITIONS
& THE RED RAG

SPECIMENS OF THE BUTTERFLY SIGNATURE
OF JAMES McNEILL WHISTLER

MR. WHISTLER'S 'TEN O'CLOCK'

LADIES AND GENTLEMEN:

It is with great hesitation and much misgiving that I appear before you, in the character of The Preacher.

If timidity be at all allied to the virtue modesty, and can find favour in your eyes, I pray you, for the sake of that virtue, accord me your utmost indulgence.

I would plead for my want of habit, did it not seem preposterous, judging from precedent, that aught save the most efficient effrontery could be ever expected in connection with my subject – for I will not conceal from you that I mean to talk about Art. Yes, Art – that has of late become, as far as much discussion and writing can make it, a sort of common topic for the tea-table.

Art is upon the Town! – to be chucked under the chin by the passing gallant – to be enticed within the gates of the householder – to be coaxed into company, as a proof of culture and refinement.

If familiarity can breed contempt, certainly Art – or what is currently taken for it – has been brought to its lowest stage of intimacy.

The people have been harassed with Art in every guise, and vexed with many methods as to its endurance. They have been told how they shall love Art, and live with it. Their homes have been invaded, their walls covered with paper, their very dress taken to task – until, roused at last, bewildered and filled with the doubts and discomforts of senseless suggestion, they resent such intrusion, and cast forth the false prophets, who have brought the very name of the beautiful into disrepute, and derision upon themselves.

Alas! ladies and gentlemen, Art has been maligned. She has naught in common with such practices. She is a goddess of dainty thought – reticent of habit, abjuring all obtrusiveness, purposing in no way to better others.

She is, withal, selfishly occupied with her own perfection only – having no desire to teach – seeking and finding the beautiful in all conditions and in all times, as did her high priest, Rembrandt, when he saw picturesque grandeur and noble dignity in the Jews' quarter of Amsterdam, and lamented not that its inhabitants were not Greeks.

As did Tintoret and Paul Veronese, among the Venetians, while not halting to change the brocaded silks for the classic draperies of Athens.

As did, at the Court of Philip, Velasquez, whose Infantas, clad in inaesthetic hoops, are, as works of Art, of the same quality as the Elgin marbles.

No reformers were these great men – no improvers of the way of others! Their productions alone were their occupation, and, filled with the poetry of their science, they required not to alter their surroundings – for, as the laws of their Art were revealed to them they saw, in the development of their work, that real beauty which, to them, was as much a matter of certainty and triumph as is to the astronomer the verification of the result, foreseen with the light given to him alone. In all this, their world was completely severed from that of their fellow-creatures with whom sentiment is mistaken for poetry; and for whom there is no perfect work that shall not be explained by the benefit conferred upon themselves.

Humanity takes the place of Art, and God's creations are excused by their usefulness. Beauty is confounded with virtue, and, before a work of Art, it is asked: 'What good shall it do?'

Hence it is that nobility of action, in this life, is hopelessly linked with the merit of the work that portrays it; and thus the people have acquired the habit of looking, as who should say, not *at* a picture, but *through* it, at some human fact, that shall, or shall not, from a social point of view, better their mental or moral state. So we have come to hear of the painting that elevates, and of the duty of the painter – of the picture that is full of thought, and of the panel that merely decorates.

A favourite faith, dear to those who teach, is that certain periods were especially artistic, and that nations, readily named, were notably lovers of Art.

So we are told that the Greeks were, as a people, worshippers of the beautiful, and that in the fifteenth century Art was engrained in the multitude.

That the great masters lived in common understanding with their patrons – that the early Italians were artists – all – and that the demand for the lovely thing produced it.

That we, of today, in gross contrast to this

Arcadian purity, call for the ungainly, and obtain the ugly.

That, could we but change our habits and climate – were we willing to wander in groves – could we be roasted out of broadcloth – were we to do without haste, and journey without speed, we should again *require* the spoon of Queen Anne, and pick at our peas with the fork of two prongs. And so, for the flock, little hamlets grow near Hammersmith, and the steam horse is scorned.

Useless! quite hopeless and false is the effort! – built upon fable, and all because 'a wise man has uttered a vain thing and filled his belly with the East wind.'

Listen! There never was an artistic period.

There never was an Art-loving nation.

In the beginning, man went forth each day – some to do battle, some to the chase; others, again, to dig and to delve in the field – all that they might gain and live, or lose and die. Until there was found among them one, differing from the rest, whose pursuits attracted him not, and so he stayed by the tents with the women, and traced strange devices with a burnt stick upon a gourd.

This man, who took no joy in the ways of his brethren – who cared not for conquest, and fretted in the field – this designer of quaint patterns – this deviser of the beautiful – who perceived in Nature about him curious curvings, as faces are seen in the fire – this dreamer apart, was the first artist.

And when, from the field and from afar, there came back the people, they took the gourd – and drank from out of it.

And presently there came to this man another – and, in time, others – of like nature, chosen by the Gods – and so they worked together; and soon they fashioned, from the moistened earth, forms resembling the gourd. And with the power of creation, the heirloom of the artist, presently they went beyond the slovenly suggestion of Nature, and the first vase was born, in beautiful proportion.

And the toilers tilled, and were athirst; and the heroes returned from fresh victories, to rejoice and to feast; and all drank alike from the artist's goblets, fashioned cunningly, taking no note the while of the craftsman's pride, and understanding not his glory in his work; drinking at the cup, not from choice, not from a consciousness that it was beautiful, but because, forsooth, there was none other!

And time, with more state, brought more capacity for luxury, and it became well that men should dwell in large houses, and rest upon couches, and eat at tables; whereupon the artist, with his artificers, built palaces, and filled them with furniture, beautiful in proportion and lovely to look upon.

And the people lived in marvels of art – and ate and drank out of masterpieces – for there was nothing else to eat and to drink out of, and no bad building to live in; no article of daily life, of luxury, or of necessity, that had not been handed down from the design of the master, and made by his workmen.

And the people questioned not, *and had nothing to say in the matter*.

So Greece was in its splendour, and Art reigned supreme – by force of fact, not by election – and there was no meddling from the outsider. The mighty warrior would no more have ventured to offer a design for the temple of Pallas Athene than would the sacred poet have proffered a plan for constructing the catapult.

And the Amateur was unknown – and the Dilettante undreamed of!

And history wrote on, and conquest accompanied civilization, and Art spread, or rather its products were carried by the victors among the vanquished from one country to another. And the customs of cultivation covered the face of the earth, so that all peoples continued to use what *the artist alone produced*.

And centuries passed in this using, and the world was flooded with all that was beautiful, until there arose a new class, who discovered the cheap, and foresaw fortune in the facture of the sham.

Then sprang into existence the tawdry, the common, the gewgaw.

The taste of the tradesman supplanted the science of the artist, and what was born of the million went back to them, and charmed them, for it was after their own heart; and the great and the small, the statesman and the slave, took to themselves the abomination that was tendered, and preferred it – and have lived with it ever since!

And the artist's occupation was gone, and the manufacturer and the huckster took his place.

And now the heroes filled from the jugs and drank from the bowls – with understanding – noting the glare of their new bravery, and taking pride in its worth.

And the people – this time – had much to say in

the matter – and all were satisfied. And Birmingham and Manchester arose in their might – and Art was relegated to the curiosity shop.

Nature contains the elements, in colour and form, of all pictures, as the keyboard contains the notes of all music.

But the artist is born to pick, and choose, and group with science, these elements, that the result may be beautiful – as the musician gathers his notes, and forms his chords, until he brings forth from chaos glorious harmony.

To say to the painter, that Nature is to be taken as she is, is to say to the player, that he may sit on the piano.

That Nature is always right, is an assertion, artistically, as untrue, as it is one whose truth is universally taken for granted. Nature is very rarely right, to such an extent even, that it might almost be said that Nature is usually wrong: that is to say, the condition of things that shall bring about the perfection of harmony worthy a picture is rare, and not common at all.

This would seem, to even the most intelligent, a doctrine almost blasphemous. So incorporated with our education has the supposed aphorism become, that its belief is held to be part of our moral being, and the words themselves have, in our ear, the ring of religion. Still, seldom does Nature succeed in producing a picture.

The sun blares, the wind blows from the east, the sky is bereft of cloud, and without, all is of iron. The windows of the Crystal Palace are seen from all points of London. The holiday-maker rejoices in the glorious day, and the painter turns aside to shut his eyes.

How little this is understood, and how dutifully the casual in Nature is accepted as sublime, may be gathered from the unlimited admiration daily produced by a very foolish sunset.

The dignity of the snow-capped mountain is lost in distinctness, but the joy of the tourist is to recognize the traveller on the top. The desire to see, for the sake of seeing it, is, with the mass, alone the one to be gratified, hence the delight in detail.

And when the evening mist clothes the riverside with poetry, as with a veil, and the poor buildings lose themselves in the dim sky, and the tall chimneys become campanili, and the warehouses are palaces in the night, and the whole city hangs in the heavens, and fairy-land is before us – then the wayfarer hastens home; the working man and the cultured one, the wise man and the one of pleasure, cease to understand, as they have ceased to see, and Nature, who, for once, has sung in tune, sings her exquisite song to the artist alone, her son and her master – her son in that he loves her, her master in that he knows her.

To him her secrets are unfolded, to him her lessons have become gradually clear. He looks at her flower, not with the enlarging lens, that he may gather facts for the botanist, but with the light of the one who sees in her choice selection of brilliant tones and delicate tints, suggestions of future harmonies.

He does not confine himself to purposeless copying, without thought, each blade of grass, as commended by the inconsequent, but, in the long curve of the narrow leaf, corrected by the straight tall stem, he learns how grace is wedded to dignity, how strength enhances sweetness, that elegance shall be the result.

In the citron wing of the pale butterfly, with its dainty spots of orange, he sees before him the stately halls of fair gold, with their slender saffron pillars, and is taught how the delicate drawing high upon the walls shall be traced in tender tones of orpiment, and repeated by the base in notes of graver hue.

In all that is dainty and lovable he finds hints for his own combinations, and *thus* is Nature ever his resource and always at his service, and to him is naught refused.

Through his brain, as through the last alembic, is distilled the refined essence of that thought which began with the Gods, and which they left him to carry out.

Set apart by them to complete their works he produces that wondrous thing called the masterpiece, which surpasses in perfection all that they have contrived in what is called Nature; and the Gods stand by and marvel, and perceive how far away more beautiful is the Venus of Melos than was their own Eve.

For some time past, the unattached writer has become the middleman in this matter of Art, and his influence, while it has widened the gulf between the people and the painter, has brought about the most complete misunderstanding as to the aim of the picture.

For him a picture is more or less a hieroglyph or symbol of story. Apart from a few technical terms, for the display of which he finds an occasion, the work is considered absolutely from a literary point of view; indeed, from what other can he consider it? And in his essays he deals with it as with a novel – a history – or an anecdote. He fails entirely and most naturally to see its excellences, or demerits – artistic – and so degrades Art, by supposing it a method of bringing about a literary climax.

It thus, in his hands, becomes merely a means of perpetrating something further, and its mission is made a secondary one, even as a means is second to an end.

The thoughts emphasized, noble or other, are inevitably attached to the incident, and become more or less noble, according to the eloquence or mental quality of the writer, who looks the while, with disdain, upon what he holds as 'mere execution' – a matter belonging, he believes, to the training of the schools, and the reward of assiduity. So that, as he goes on with his translation from canvas to paper, the work becomes his own. He finds poetry where he would feel it were he himself transcribing the event, invention in the intricacy of the *mise en scène*, and noble philosophy in some detail of philanthropy, courage, modesty, or virtue, suggested to him by the occurrence.

All this might be brought before him, and his imagination be appealed to, by a very poor picture – indeed, I might safely say that it generally is.

Meanwhile, the *painter's* poetry is quite lost to him – the amazing invention that shall have put form and colour into such perfect harmony, that exquisiteness is the result, he is without understanding – the nobility of thought, that shall have given the artist's dignity to the whole, says to him absolutely nothing.

So that his praises are published, for virtues we would blush to possess – while the great qualities, that distinguish the one work from the thousand, that make of the masterpiece the thing of beauty that it is – have never been seen at all.

That this is so, we can make sure of, by looking back at old reviews upon past exhibitions, and reading the flatteries lavished upon men who have since been forgotten altogether – but, upon whose works, the language has been exhausted, in rhapsodies – that left nothing for the National Gallery.

A curious matter, in its effect upon the judgement of these gentlemen, is the accepted vocabulary of poetic symbolism, that helps them, by habit, in dealing with Nature: a mountain, to them, is synonymous with height – a lake, with depth – the ocean, with vastness – the sun, with glory.

So that a picture with a mountain, a lake, and an ocean – however poor in paint – is inevitably 'lofty,' 'vast,' 'infinite,' and 'glorious' – on paper.

There are those also, sombre of mien, and wise with the wisdom of books, who frequent museums and burrow in crypts; collecting – comparing – compiling – classifying – contradicting.

Experts these – for whom a date is an accomplishment – a hall-mark, success!

Careful in scrutiny are they, and conscientious of judgement – establishing, with due weight, unimportant reputations – discovering the picture, by the stain on the back – testing the torso, by the leg that is missing – filling folios with doubts on the way of that limb – disputations and dictatorial, concerning the birthplace of inferior persons – speculating, in much writing, upon the great worth of bad work.

True clerks of the collection, they mix memoranda with ambition, and, reducing Art to statistics, they 'file' the fifteenth century, and 'pigeon-hole' the antique!

Then the Preacher 'appointed'!

He stands in high places – harangues and holds forth.

Sage of the Universities – learned in many matters, and of much experience in all, save his subject.

Exhorting – denouncing – directing.

Filled with wrath and earnestness.

Bringing powers of persuasion, and polish of language, to prove – nothing.

Torn with much teaching – having naught to impart.

Impressive – important – shallow

Defiant – distressed – desperate.

Crying out, and cutting himself – while the gods hear not.

Gentle priest of the Philistine withal, again he ambles pleasantly from all point, and through many volumes, escaping scientific assertion – 'babbles of green fields.'

So Art has become foolishly confounded with education – that all should be equally qualified.

Whereas, while polish, refinement, culture, and breeding, are in no way arguments for artistic result, it is also no reproach to the most finished scholar or greatest gentleman in the land that he be absolutely without eye for painting or ear for music – that in his heart he prefers the popular print to the scratch of Rembrandt's needle, or the songs of the hall to Beethoven's 'C minor Symphony.'

Let him have but the wit to say so, and not feel the admission a proof of inferiority.

Art happens – no hovel is safe from it, no Prince may depend upon it, the vastest intelligence cannot bring it about, and puny efforts to make it universal end in quaint comedy, and coarse farce.

This is as it should be – and all attempts to make it otherwise are due to the eloquence of the ignorant, the zeal of the conceited.

The boundary-line is clear. Far from me to propose to bridge it over – that the pestered people be pushed across. No! I would save them from further fatigue. I would come to their relief, and would lift from their shoulders this incubus of Art.

Why, after centuries of freedom from it, and indifference to it, should it now be thrust upon them by the blind – until wearied and puzzled, they know no longer how they shall eat or drink – how they shall sit or stand – or wherewithal they shall clothe themselves – without afflicting Art.

But, lo! there is much talk without!

Triumphantly they cry, 'Beware! This matter does indeed concern us. We also have our part in all true Art! – for, remember the "one touch of Nature" that "makes the whole world kin." '

True, indeed. But let not the unwary jauntily suppose that Shakespeare herewith hands him his passport to Paradise, and thus permits him speech among the chosen. Rather, learn that, in this very sentence, he is condemned to remain without – to continue with the common.

This one chord that vibrates with all – this 'one touch of Nature' that calls aloud to the response of each – that explains the popularity of the 'Bull' of Paul Potter – that excuses the price of Murillo's 'Conception' – this one unspoken sympathy that pervades humanity, is – Vulgarity!

Vulgarity – under whose fascinating influence 'the many' have elbowed 'the few,' and the gentle circle of Art swarms with the intoxicated mob of mediocrity, whose leaders prate and counsel, and call aloud, where the Gods once spoke in whisper!

And now from their midst the Dilettante stalks abroad. The amateur is loosed The voice of the aesthete is heard in the land, and catastrophe is upon us.

The meddler beckons the vengeance of the Gods, and ridicule threatens the fair daughters of the land.

And there are curious converts to a weird *culte*, in which all instinct for attractiveness – all freshness and sparkle – all woman's winsomeness – is to give way to a strange vocation for the unlovely – and this desecration in the name of the Graces!

Shall this gaunt, ill-at-ease, distressed, abashed mixture of *mauvaise honte* and desperate assertion call itself artistic, and claim cousinship with the artist – who delights in the dainty, the sharp, bright gaiety of beauty?

No! – a thousand times no! Here are no connections of ours.

We will have nothing to do with them.

Forced to seriousness, that emptiness may be hidden, they dare not smile –

While the artist, in fulness of heart and head, is glad, and laughs aloud, and is happy in his strength, and is merry at the pompous pretension – the solemn silliness that surrounds him.

For Art and Joy go together, with bold openness, and high head, and ready hand – fearing naught, and dreading no exposure.

Know, then, all beautiful women, that we are with you. Pay no need, we pray you, to this outcry of the unbecoming – this last plea for the plain.

It concerns you not.

Your own instinct is near the truth – your own wit far surer guide than the untaught ventures of thick-heeled Apollos.

What! will you up and follow the first piper that leads you down Petticoat Lane, there, on a Sabbath, to gather, for the week, from the dull rags of ages wherewith to bedeck yourselves? that, beneath your travestied awkwardness, we have trouble to find your own dainty selves? Oh, fie! Is the world, then exhausted? and must we go back because the thumb of the mountebank jerks the other way?

Costume is not dress.

And the wearers of wardrobes may not be doctors of taste!

For by what authority shall these be pretty masters? Look well, and nothing have they invented – nothing put together for comeliness' sake.

Haphazard from their shoulders hang the garments of the hawker – combining in their person the motley of many manners with the medley of the mummers' closet.

Set up as a warning, and a finger-post of danger, they point to the disastrous effect of Art upon the middle classes.

Why this lifting of the brow in deprecation of the present – this pathos in reference to the past?

If Art be rare today, it was seldom heretofore.

It is false, this teaching of decay.

The master stands in no relation to the moment at which he occurs – a monument of isolation – hinting at sadness – having no part in the progress of his fellow-men.

He is also no more the product of civilization than is the scientific truth asserted dependent upon the wisdom of a period. The assertion itself requires the *man* to make it. The truth was from the beginning.

So Art is limited to the infinite, and beginning there cannot progress.

A silent indication of its wayward independence from all extraneous advance, is in the absolutely unchanged condition and form of implement since the beginning of things.

The painter has but the same pencil – the sculptor the chisel of centuries.

Colours are not more since the heavy hangings of night were first drawn aside, and the loveliness of light revealed.

Neither chemist nor engineer can offer new elements of the masterpiece.

False again, the fabled link between the grandeur of Art and the glories and virtues of the State, for Art feeds not upon nations, and peoples may be wiped from the face of the earth, but Art *is*.

It is indeed high time that we cast aside the weary weight of responsibility and co-partnership, and know that, in no way, do our virtues minister to its worth, in no way do our vices impede its triumph!

How irksome! how hopeless! how superhuman the self-imposed task of the nation! How sublimely vain the belief that it shall live nobly or art perish.

Let us reassure ourselves, at our own option is our virtue. Art we in no way affect.

A whimsical goddess, and a capricious, her strong sense of joy tolerates no dulness, and, live we never so spotlessly, still may she turn her back upon us.

As, from time immemorial, she has done upon the Swiss in their mountains.

What more worthy people! Whose every Alpine gap yawns with tradition, and is stocked with noble story; yet, the perverse and scornful one will none of it, and the sons of patriots are left with the clock that turns the mill, and the sudden cuckoo, with difficulty restrained in its box.

For this was Tell a hero! For this did Gessler die!

Art, the cruel jade, cares not, and hardens her heart, and hies her off to the East, to find, among the opium-eaters of Nankin, a favourite with whom she lingers fondly – caressing his blue porcelain, and painting his coy maidens, and marking his plates with her six marks of choice – indifferent in her companionship with him, to all save the virtue of his refinement!

He it is who calls her – he who holds her!

And again to the West, that her next lover may bring together the Gallery at Madrid, and show to the world how the Master towers above all; and in their intimacy they revel, he and she, in this knowledge; and he knows the happiness untasted by other mortal.

She is proud of her comrade, and promises that in after-years, others shall pass that way, and understand.

So in all time does this superb one cast about for the man worthy her love – and Art seeks the Artist alone.

Where he is, there she appears, and remains with him – loving and fruitful – turning never aside in moments of hope deferred – of insult – and of ribald misunderstanding; and when he dies she sadly takes her flight, though loitering yet in the land, from fond association, but refusing to be consoled.*

With the man, then, and not with the multitude, are her intimacies; and in the book of her life the names inscribed are few – scant, indeed, the list of those who have helped to write her story of love and beauty.

From the sunny morning, when, with her glorious Greek relenting, she yielded up the secret of repeated line, as, with his hand in hers, together they marked in marble, the measured rhyme of lovely limb and draperies flowing in unison, to the day when she dipped the Spaniard's brush in light

*And so have we the ephemeral influence of the Master's memory – the afterglow, in which are warmed, for a while, the worker and disciple.

and air, and made his people live within their frames, and *stand upon their legs*, that all nobility and sweetness, and tenderness, and magnificence should be theirs by right, ages had gone by, and few had been her choice.

Countless, indeed, the horde of pretenders! But she knew them not.

A teeming, seething, busy mass, whose virtue was industry, and whose industry was vice!

Their names go to fill the catalogue of the collection at home, of the gallery abroad, for the delectation of the bagman and the critic.

Therefore have we cause to be merry! – and to cast away all care – resolved that all is well – as it ever was – and that it is not meet that we should be cried at, and urged to take measures!

Enough have we endured of dulness! Surely are we weary of weeping, and our tears have been cozened from us falsely, for they have called out woe! when there was no grief – and, alas! where all is fair!

We have then but to wait – until, with the mark of the Gods upon him – there come among us again the chosen – who shall continue what has gone before. Satisfied that, even were he never to appear, the story of the beautiful is already complete – hewn in the marbles of the Parthenon – and broidered, with the birds, upon the fan of Hokusai – at the foot of Fusiyama.

Delivered in London Feb. 20, 1885

Propositions – No. 2

A PICTURE is finished when all trace of the means used to bring about the end has disappeared.

To say of a picture, as is often said in its praise, that it shows great and earnest labour, is to say that it is incomplete and unfit for view.

Industry in Art is a necessity – not a virtue – and any evidence of the same, in the production, is a blemish, not a quality; a proof, not of achievement, but of absolutely insufficient work, for work alone will efface the footsteps of work.

The work of the master reeks not of the sweat of the brow – suggests no effort – and is finished from its beginning.

The completed task of perseverance only, has never been begun, and will remain unfinished to eternity – a monument of goodwill and foolishness.

'There is one that laboureth, and taketh pains, and maketh haste, and is so much the more behind.'

The masterpiece should appear as the flower to the painter – perfect in its bud as in its bloom – with no reason to explain its presence – no mission to fulfil – a joy to the artist – a delusion to the philanthropist – a puzzle to the botanist – an accident of sentiment and alliteration to the literary man.

A Further Proposition

THE notion that I paint flesh lower in tone than it is in nature, is entirely based upon the popular superstition as to what flesh really is –when seen on canvas; for the people never look at nature with any sense of its pictorial appearance – for which reason, by the way, they also never look at a picture with any sense of nature, but, unconsciously from habit, with reference to what they have seen in other pictures.

Now, in the usual 'pictures of the year' there is but one flesh, that shall do service under all circumstances, whether the person painted be in the soft light of the room or out in the glare of the open. The one aim of the unsuspecting painter is to make his man 'stand out' from the frame – never doubting that, on the contrary, he should really, and in truth absolutely does, stand *within* the frame – and at a depth behind it equal to the distance at which the painter sees his model. The frame is, indeed, the window through which the painter looks at his model, and nothing could be more offensively inartistic than this brutal attempt to thrust the model on the hitherside of this window!

Yet this is the false condition of things to which all have become accustomed, and in the stupendous effort to bring it about, exaggeration has been exhausted – and the traditional means of the incompetent can no further go.

Lights have been heightened until the white of the tube alone remains – shadows have been deepened until black alone is left. Scarcely a feature stays in its place, so fierce is its intention of 'firmly' coming forth; and in the midst of this unseemly struggle for prominence, the gentle truth has but a sorry chance, falling flat and flavourless, and without force.

The Master from Madrid, himself, beside this monster success of mediocrity, would be looked upon as mild: *beau bien sure, mais pas 'dans le mouvement'* !

Whereas, could the people be induced to turn their eyes but for a moment, with the fresh power of comparison, upon their fellow-creatures as they pass in the gallery, they might be made dimly to perceive (though I doubt it, so blind is their belief in the bad).

The Red Rag

WHY should not I call my works 'symphonies,' 'arrangements,' 'harmonies,' and 'nocturnes'? I know that many good people think my nomenclature funny and myself 'eccentric.' Yes, 'eccentric' is the adjective they find for me.

The vast majority of English folk cannot and will not consider a picture as a picture, apart from any story which it may be supposed to tell.

My picture of a 'Harmony in Grey and Gold' is an illustration of my meaning – a snow scene with a single black figure and a lighted tavern. I care nothing for the past, present, or future of the black figure, placed there because the black was wanted at that spot. All that I know is that my combination of grey and gold is the basis of the picture. Now this is precisely what my friends cannot grasp.

They say, 'Why not call it "Trotty Veck," and sell it for a round harmony of golden guineas?' – naïvely acknowledging that, without baptism, there is no . . . market!

But even commercially this stocking of your shop with the goods of another would be indecent – custom alone has made it dignified. Not even the popularity of Dickens should be invoked to lend an adventitious aid to art of another kind from his. I should hold it a vulgar and meretricious trick to excite people about Trotty Veck when, if they really could care for pictorial art at all, they would know that the picture should have its own merit, and not depend upon dramatic, or legendary, or local interest.

As music is the poetry of sound, so is painting the poetry of sight, and the subject-matter has nothing to do with harmony of sound or of colour.

The great musicians knew this. Beethoven and the rest wrote music – simply music; symphony in this key, concerto or sonata in that.

On F or G they constructed celestial harmonies – as harmonies – as combinations, evolved from the chords of F or G and their minor correlatives.

This is pure music as distinguished from airs – commonplace and vulgar in themselves, but interesting from their associations, as, for instance, 'Yankee Doodle,' or 'Partant pour la Syrie.'

Art should be independent of all clap-trap – should stand alone, and appeal to the artistic sense of eye or ear, without confounding this with emotions entirely foreign to it, as devotion, pity, love, patriotism, and the like. All these have no kind of concern with it, and that is why I insist on calling my works 'arrangements' and 'harmonies.'

Take the picture of my mother, exhibited at the Royal Academy as an 'Arrangement in Grey and Black.' Now that is what it is. To me it is interesting as a picture of my mother; but what can or ought the public to care about the identity of the portrait?

The imitator is a poor kind of creature. If the man who paints only the tree, or flower, or other surface he sees before him were an artist, the king of artists would be the photographer. It is for the artist to do something beyond this: in portrait painting to put on canvas something more than the face the model wears for that one day; to paint the man, in short, as well as his features; in arrangement of colours to treat a flower as his key, not as his model.

This is now understood indifferently well – at least by dressmakers. In every costume you see attention is paid to the key-note of colour which runs through the composition, as the chant of the Anabaptists through the *Prophète*, or the Huguenots' hymn in the opera of that name.

THE PLATES

1. SELF-PORTRAIT. About 1857-8. Washington, Freer Gallery of Art

2. LA MÈRE GÉRARD. After 1855. Dublin, E. Swift Newton

3. HEAD OF AN OLD MAN SMOKING. After 1855. Paris, Louvre

4. A STREET AT SAVERNE. Etching. 1858

5. THE LIME BURNER. Etching. 1859

6. THE MUSIC ROOM. Etching. About 1859

7. AT THE PIANO. Begun 1858. Cincinnati, Art Museum

8. FINETTE. Etching. 1859

9. HARMONY IN GREEN AND ROSE: THE MUSIC ROOM. 1860. Washington, Freer Gallery of Art

10. BLACK LION WHARF. Etching. 1859

11. WAPPING. 1861–4. New York, Mr. and Mrs. John Hay Whitney

12. DETAIL OF PLATE 11

13. THE THAMES IN ICE: THE 25TH DECEMBER 1860. Washington, Freer Gallery of Art

14. THE LITTLE POOL. Etching. 1861

15. 'SOUPE À TROIS SOUS'. Etching. About 1861

16. ROTHERHITHE – WAPPING. Etching. 1860

17. THE STORM. Etching. 1861

18. THE COAST OF BRITTANY – ALONE WITH THE TIDE. 1861. Hartford, Conn., Wadsworth Atheneum

19. THE BLUE WAVE: BIARRITZ. 1862. Farmington, Conn., Hillstead Museum

20. BROWN AND SILVER: OLD BATTERSEA BRIDGE. First Exhibited 1865. Andover, Mass., Addison Gallery of American Art

21. BATTERSEA REACH. About 1863–4. Washington, Corcoran Gallery of Art

22. THE LAST OF OLD WESTMINSTER. 1862. Boston, Museum of Fine Arts

23. DETAIL OF PLATE 20

24. DETAIL OF PLATE 22

25. SYMPHONY IN WHITE NO. 1: THE WHITE GIRL. 1862. Washington, National Gallery of Art

26. ROSE AND SILVER: 'LA PRINCESSE DU PAYS DE LA PORCELAINE'. 1864. Washington, Freer Gallery of Art

27. SLEEPING WOMAN. Drawing. About 1862–3. Washington, National Gallery of Art

28. PURPLE AND ROSE: THE LANGE LIJZEN OF THE SIX MARKS. 1864. Philadelphia, Museum of Art, John G. Johnson Collection

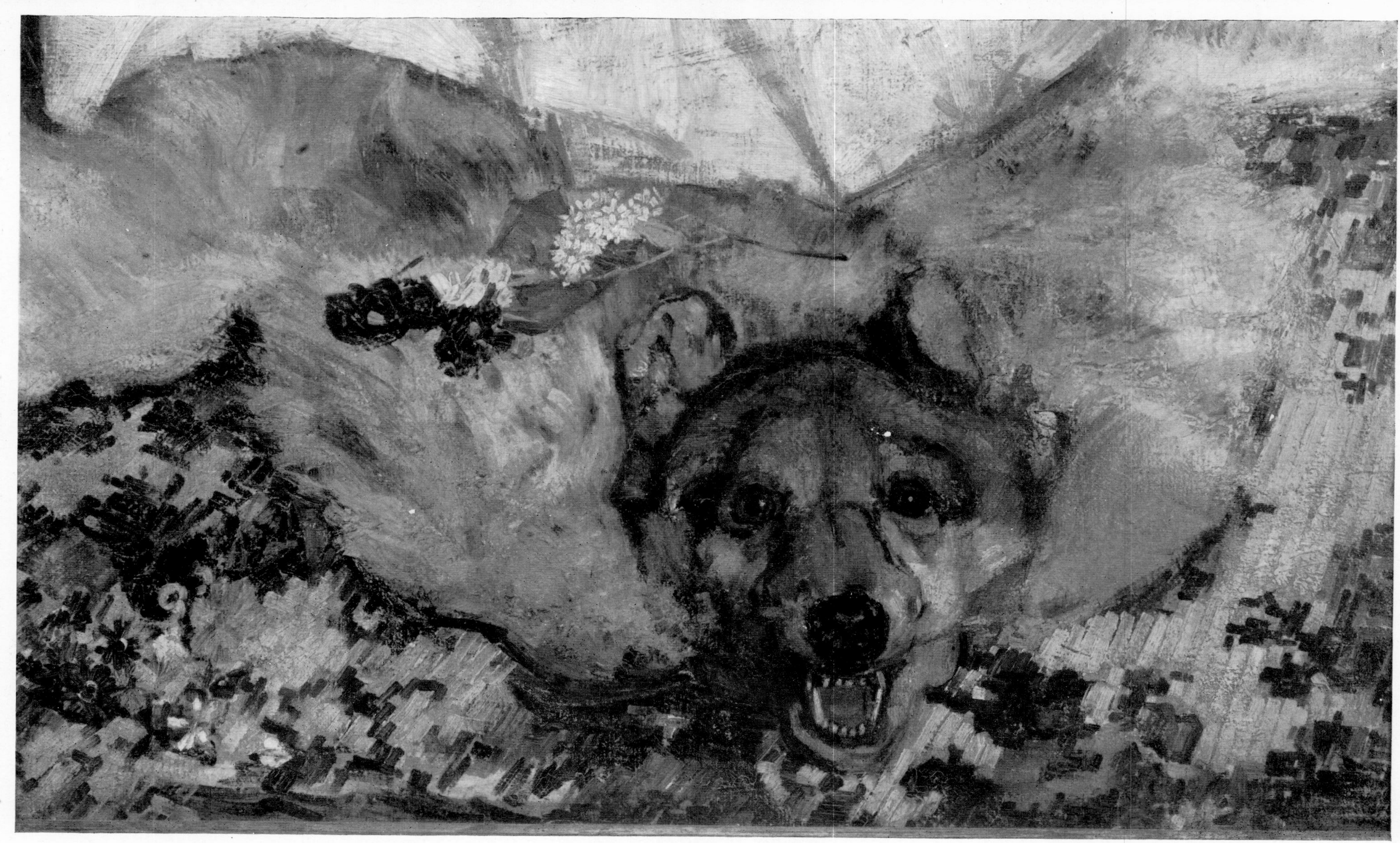

29. DETAIL OF PLATE 25

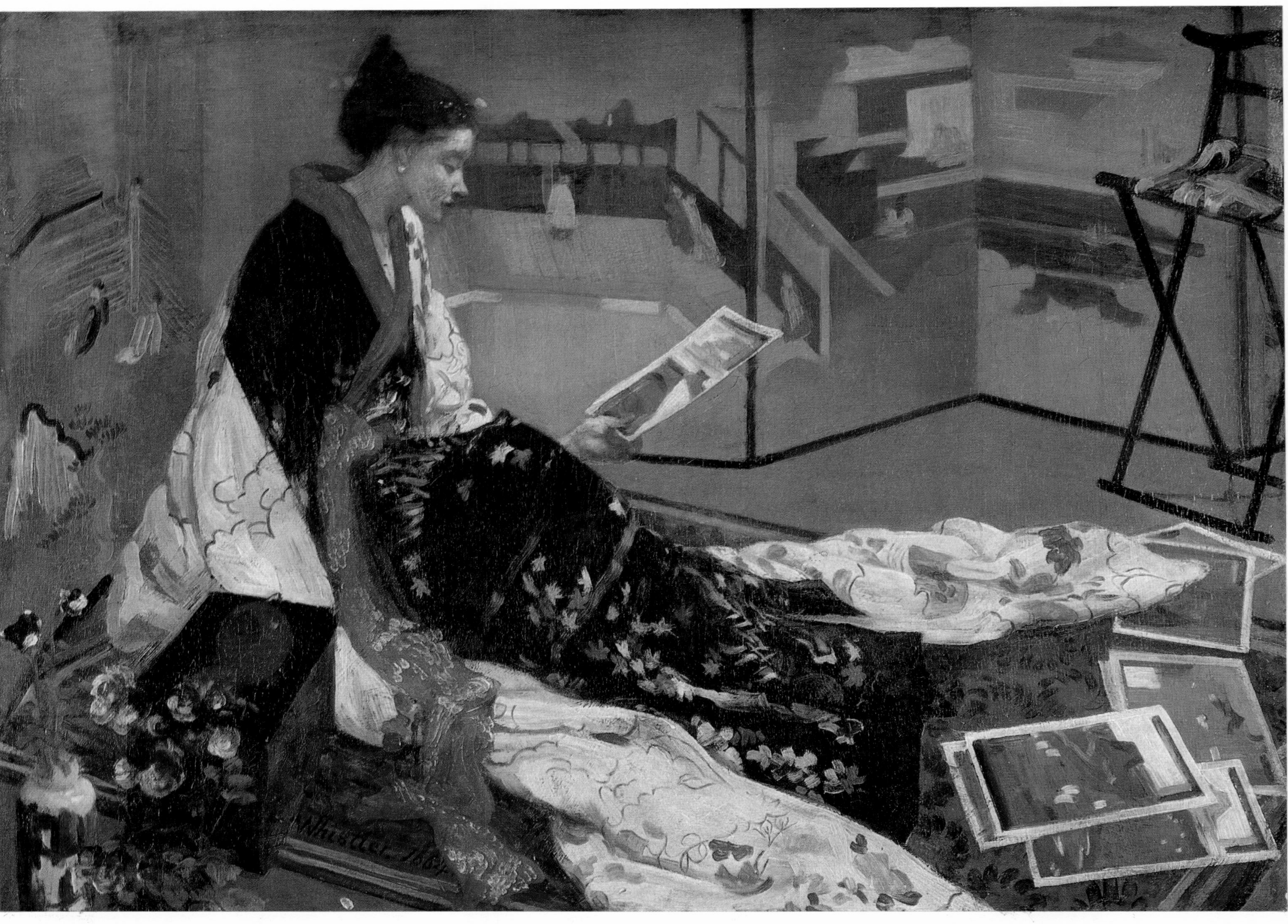

30. CAPRICE IN PURPLE AND GOLD. NO. 2: THE GOLDEN SCREEN. 1864. Washington, Freer Gallery of Art

31. DETAIL OF PLATE 30

32. DETAIL OF FRONTISPIECE

33. HARMONY IN BLUE AND SILVER: TROUVILLE. 1865. Boston, Isabella Stewart Gardner Museum

34. HARMONY IN GREY: CHELSEA IN ICE. About 1864. London, Private Collection

35. CREPUSCULE IN FLESH COLOUR AND GREEN: VALPARAISO. 1866. London, Tate Gallery

36. SYMPHONY IN GREY AND GREEN: THE OCEAN. About 1866–7. New York, Frick Collection

37. NOCTURNE IN BLUE AND GOLD: VALPARAISO. 1866. Washington, Freer Gallery of Art

38. DESIGN FOR A MOSAIC. About 1873. Private Collection

39. ANNABEL LEE. Pastel. 1860's. Washington, Freer Gallery of Art

40. SYMPHONY IN WHITE NO. 3. 1867. Birmingham, Barber Institute of Fine Arts

41. THREE FIGURES: PINK AND GREY. About 1868. London, Tate Gallery

42. SYMPHONY IN BLUE AND PINK. About 1868. Washington, Freer Gallery of Art

43. VARIATIONS IN BLUE AND GREEN. About 1868. Washington, Freer Gallery of Art

44. VARIATIONS IN FLESH-COLOUR AND GREEN: THE BALCONY. About 1867–8. Washington, Freer Gallery of Art

45. THE ARTIST'S STUDIO. About 1867–8. Chicago, Art Institute

46. DETAIL OF PLATE 44

47. DETAIL OF PLATE 40

48. TWO FEMALE FIGURES. Drawing. About 1868. Cambridge, Mass., Fogg Art Museum

49. VENUS RISING FROM THE SEA. About 1868. Washington, Freer Gallery of Art

50. SPEKE HALL. Etching. 1870.

51. VARIATIONS IN VIOLET AND GREEN. 1871. U.S.A., Private Collection

52. A GIRL READING. Drawing. 1870's. Glasgow University, Birnie Philip Gift

53. ARRANGEMENT IN GREY AND BLACK NO. 1: THE ARTIST'S MOTHER. First exhibited 1872. Paris, Louvre

54. DETAIL OF PLATE 57

55. DETAIL OF PLATE 53

56. HARMONY IN GREY AND GREEN: MISS CICELY ALEXANDER. About 1872–4. London, Tate Gallery

57. ARRANGEMENT IN GREY AND BLACK NO. 2: THOMAS CARLYLE. 1872–73. Glasgow, City Art Gallery and Museum

58. DETAIL OF PLATE 56

59. ARRANGEMENT IN GREY: SELF-PORTRAIT. Between 1871 and 1873. Detroit, Institute of Arts

60. ARRANGEMENT IN BLACK: PORTRAIT OF F. R. LEYLAND. 1873. Washington, Freer Gallery of Art

61. SYMPHONY IN FLESH COLOUR AND PINK: MRS. F. R. LEYLAND. 1873. New York, Frick Collection

62. ARRANGEMENT IN BLACK AND WHITE: THE YOUNG AMERICAN. First exhibited 1874. Washington, Freer Gallery of Art

63. THE WHITE GIRL NO. 4. First exhibited 1874. Cambridge, Mass., Fogg Art Museum

64. NOCTURNE IN BLUE AND SILVER: CREMORNE LIGHTS. 1872. London, Tate Gallery

65. NOCTURNE IN BLUE AND GREEN: CHELSEA. 1871. London, Miss J. Alexander

66. NOCTURNE IN BLUE AND GOLD: OLD BATTERSEA BRIDGE. About 1872–75. London, Tate Gallery

67. NOCTURNE IN BLACK AND GOLD: THE FIRE WHEEL. About 1874–75. London, Tate Gallery

68. CREMORNE GARDENS NO. 2. About 1875. New York, Metropolitan Museum

69. DETAIL OF PLATE 68

70. NOCTURNE IN BLACK AND GOLD: THE FALLING ROCKET. About 1874. Detroit, Institute of Art

71. ARRANGEMENT IN BLACK AND BROWN: ROSA CORDER. About 1876. New York, Frick Collection

72. ARRANGEMENT IN BLACK AND BROWN: THE FUR JACKET. First exhibited 1877. Worcester, Mass., Art Museum

73. HARMONY IN YELLOW AND GOLD: THE GOLD GIRL, CONNIE GILCHRIST. About 1876. New York, Metropolitan Museum

74. ARRANGEMENT IN YELLOW AND GREY: EFFIE DEANS. 1876. Amsterdam, Rijksmuseum

75. STUDY FOR THE PORTRAIT OF MRS. LOUIS HUTH. Drawing. 1870's. Oxford, Ashmolean Museum

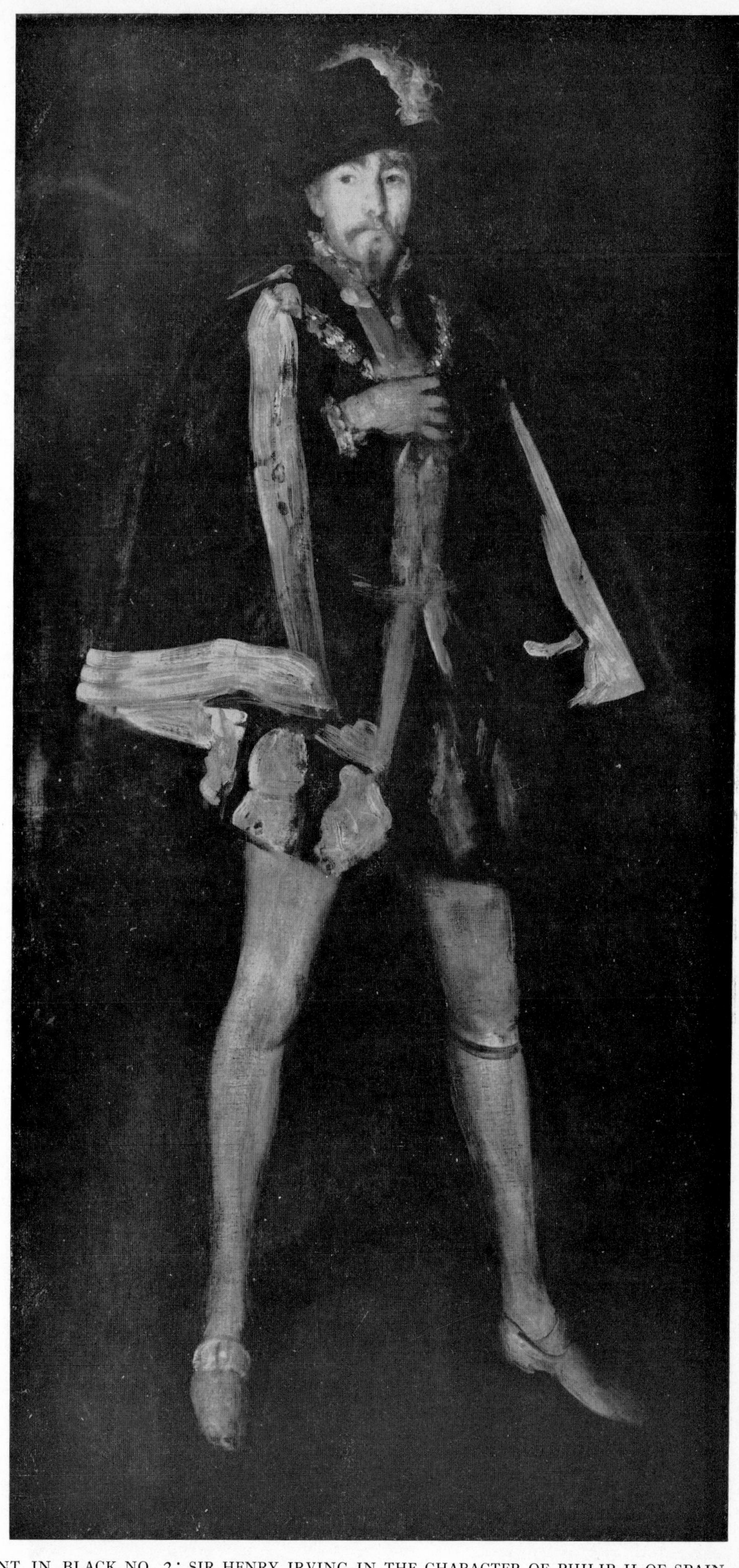

76. ARRANGEMENT IN BLACK NO. 3: SIR HENRY IRVING IN THE CHARACTER OF PHILIP II OF SPAIN IN TENNYSON'S 'QUEEN MARY'. Begun 1876, reworked later. New York, Metropolitan Museum

81. NOCTURNE: CREMORNE GARDENS, NO. 3. Between 1875 and 1877. Washington, Freer Gallery of Art

77. NOC

78. NO

82. GREY AND SILVER: THE ANGRY SEA. First exhibited 1884. Washington, Freer Gallery of Art

83. NOCTURNE IN BLACK AND GOLD: ENTRANCE TO SOUTHAMPTON WATERS. Late 1870's to early 1880's. Chicago, Art Institute

84. NOCTURNE IN BLUE AND SILVER: THE LAGOON, VENICE. About 1880. Boston, Museum of Fine Art

85. THE MAST. Etching. 1880

86. ALLEY IN VENICE. Pastel. 1880. Cambridge, Mass., Fogg Art Museum

87. THE BALCONY. Etching. 1880

88. NOCTURNE: PALACES. Etching. 1879–80

89. RIVA DEGLI SCHIAVONI AT SUNSET. Pastel. 1880. Cambridge, Mass., Fogg Art Museum

90. STORMY SUNSET. Pastel. 1880. Cambridge, Mass., Fogg Art Museum

91. HARMONY IN FLESH COLOUR AND PINK: LADY MEUX. 1881. New York, Frick Collection

92. ARRANGEMENT IN FLESH COLOUR AND BLACK: PORTRAIT OF THÉODORE DURET. 1882–84. New York, Metropolitan Museum

93. ARRANGEMENT IN BLACK: LADY IN A YELLOW BUSKIN – LADY ARCHIBALD CAMPBELL.
First exhibited in 1884. Philadelphia, Museum of Art, Wilstach Collection

94. ROSE AND SILVER: PORTRAIT OF MRS. WHIBLEY. Watercolour. 1890's. Washington, Freer Gallery of Art

95. ARRANGEMENT IN BLACK: PABLO DE SARASATE. 1884. Pittsburgh, Carnegie Institute

96. HARMONY IN RED: LAMPLIGHT – MRS. WHISTLER. First exhibited in 1886. Glasgow University, Birnie Philip Gift

97. GREEN AND VIOLET: MRS. WALTER SICKERT. 1885. Cambridge, Mass., Fogg Art Museum

98. PORTRAIT OF GEORGE A. LUCAS. 1886. Baltimore, Walters Art Gallery

99. THE ARTIST'S MODEL MAUD READING IN BED. Watercolour. Baltimore, Walters Art Gallery

100. THE GOLD RUFF. Glasgow University, Birnie Philip Gift

101. GOLD AND ORANGE: THE NEIGHBOURS. 1880's. Washington, Freer Gallery of Art

102. 'UNE PETITE BONNE À LA PORTE D'UNE AUBERGE.' Late 1890's. New Orleans, Mr. and Mrs. Charles C. Henderson

103. CHELSEA SHOPS. Early 1880's. Washington, Freer Gallery of Art

104. A NOTE IN RED. 1880's. Washington, Freer Gallery of Art

105. SOUTHEND PIER. Watercolour. Late 1880's. Washington, Freer Gallery of Art

106. RANELAGH GARDENS. Watercolour. 1880's or 1890's. Washington, Freer Gallery of Art

107. THE STEPS – LUXEMBOURG GARDENS. Lithograph. 1894

108. THE EMBROIDERED CURTAIN. Etching. 1889

109. THE GREENGROCER'S SHOP. (Unfinished.) 1893–5. Glasgow University, Birnie Philip Gift

110. DORSETSHIRE LANDSCAPE. 1895. Washington, Freer Gallery of Art

III. THE LITTLE GREEN CAP. Washington, Freer Gallery of Art

112. LITTLE ROSE OF LYME REGIS. 1895. Boston, Museum of Fine Arts

113. THE DUET. Lithograph. 1894

114. MRS. CHARLES WHIBLEY READING. 1894. Glasgow University, Birnie Philip Bequest

115. PURPLE AND GOLD: PHRYNE THE SUPERB, BUILDER OF TEMPLES. 1898. Washington, Freer Gallery of Art

116. ROSE AND BROWN: LA CIGALE. First exhibited in 1899. Washington, Freer Gallery of Art

117. A SEATED GIRL HOLDING A BABY. Pastel. Late 1890's Glasgow University, Birnie Philip Gift

118. VENUS ASTARTE. Pastel. Late 1890's. Washington, Freer Gallery of Art

119. GREY AND GOLD: THE GOLDEN BAY, IRELAND. 1900. Private Collection

120. AJACCIO, CORSICA. 1901. Cambridge, Mass., Fogg Art Museum

121. ARRANGEMENT IN BLACK AND GOLD: COMTE ROBERT DE MONTESQUIOU. 1891. New York, Frick Collection

122. PORTRAIT OF A. J. EDDY. Begun 1894. Chicago, Art Institute

123. PORTRAIT OF GEORGE W. VANDERBILT. Begun 1897. Washington, National Gallery of Art

124. GOLD AND BROWN: SELF-PORTRAIT. About 1898. Glasgow University, Birnie Philip Gift

125. PORTRAIT SKETCH OF A LADY. Washington, Freer Gallery of Art

126. PORTRAIT OF CHARLES L. FREER. About 1902. Washington, Freer Gallery of Art

127. DOROTHY SEATON: A DAUGHTER OF EVE. 1902. Glasgow University, Birnie Philip Gift

128. GOLD AND BROWN: SELF-PORTRAIT. About 1900. Washington, National Gallery of Art

129. DETAIL OF FRONTISPIECE

NOTES ON THE PLATES

WHISTLER IN HIS FULHAM ROAD STUDIO

NOTES ON THE PLATES

(A Bibliographical Note on page 199 explains the abbreviated references used in these notes)

Frontispiece: SYMPHONY IN WHITE NO. 2: THE LITTLE WHITE GIRL. Canvas. 76×51 cm. Signed Whistler. London, Tate Gallery.

The model is Joanna Heffernan (Mrs. Abbott), the artist's Irish model and mistress. Painted in 1864, this famous picture was exhibited at the Royal Academy in the same year. It inspired Swinburne to write the poem 'Before the Mirror: Verses under a Picture', an extract from which was pasted by the artist onto the frame. Later this picture was shown at Goupil's in 1892, at the 1895 International Exhibition at Venice, in the Exposition Universelle in Paris in 1900, and at the Royal Scottish Academy, Edinburgh, 1902. When shown in Paris, Gustave Geffroy wrote: 'Il est enfin, dans la section americaine, un grande artiste qui a eu l'influence la plus étendue et la plus profonde non seulement sur le nouveau monde, mais aussi sur l'ancien. James MacNeill Whistler, peintre égal aux plus savants, poète admirable de la vie spirituelle, étrange, mysterieux, distingué, à la façon de Velazquez et d'Edgar Poe.' *La Vie Artistique*, vol. VII, 1901, p. 200.

1. SELF-PORTRAIT. Canvas. 46·3×38·1 cm. Signed Whistler. Washington, Freer Gallery of Art.

According to the Catalogue of the Paris Memorial Exhibition of 1905, this was painted in about 1857–58. It reflects the artist's desire to emulate the Bohemianism of Henry Murger and his affinities with the current Realist movement in Paris. It may also suggest an awareness of Rembrandt's early self-portraits. Whistler gave it to his friend, the artist Ernest Delannoy. It was bought by Freer from Samuel P. Avery in 1871.

2. LA MÈRE GÉRARD. Oil on board. 28×20 cm. Dublin, E. Swift Newton.

According to the Pennells, quoting Whistler (*Life*, I, p. 57) this was the first picture the artist painted after his arrival in Paris in 1855. The sitter was an old seller of violets and matches stationed in the Luxembourg Gardens. This picture was exhibited at the Royal Academy in 1861 and once belonged to A. C. Swinburne, of whom Whistler made a print (Fig. 25), then to Theodore Watts Dunton and William Heinemann. There are apparently two other versions of the picture, one of which seems to have belonged to Charles Drouet (1836–1908), of whom he made a drypoint. Whistler made two etchings of La Mère Gérard (K. 11 and 12).

3. HEAD OF AN OLD MAN SMOKING. Canvas. 41×33 cm. Signed Whistler. Paris, Louvre.

Pennell, *Life* I, p. 74, stated that the model was an old man, a pedlar of crockery, the artist had noticed in Les Halles. It indicates the influence of Courbet on Whistler in the late 1850's. It belonged to the artist's friend Charles Drouet (1836–1908), of whom he made a drypoint; Drouet bequeathed it to the Luxembourg Museum, Paris.

4. A STREET AT SAVERNE. Etching. 20·8×15·7 cm. K. 19.

No. 6 of the *Twelve Etchings from Nature* (*The French Set*). Saverne is a town in Alsace which is now called Zabern.

5. THE LIME BURNER. Etching. 25×17·6 cm. K. 46. 1859.

No. 9 of *A Series of Sixteen Etchings of Scenes on the Thames and other Subjects* (*The Thames Set*). An impression was exhibited at the Royal Academy in 1860.

6. THE MUSIC ROOM. Etching. 14·5×21·7 cm. K. 33. About 1859.

Deborah Haden and her husband. The man behind the table is Haden's assistant, James Traer.

7. AT THE PIANO. Canvas. 66×90 cm. Signed Whistler. Cincinnati, Art Museum.

The sitters are the artist's half-sister Deborah Haden, the wife of Sir F. Seymour Haden and their daughter Annie (later Mrs. Charles Thynne) of whom the artist made a number of etchings. The picture was started in November 1858. It was rejected at the Salon of 1859 but exhibited in the studio of François Bonvin in the Rue St. Jacques, Paris, and was admired there by Courbet. It was exhibited at the Royal Academy in 1860 and bought by John Philip, the Royal Academician, who specialised in Spanish scenes. It was later shown at the Salons of 1867 and 1883, at the Pennsylvanian Academy, 1881, the Society of American Artists, New York, 1882, and at the International Society, London, 1898.

8. FINETTE. Etching. 28·8×20·1 cm. K. 58. 1859.

She was a cocotte and a dancer, generally the companion of Alice la Provençale or of Rigolbache, in a famous quadrille then in vogue. She later came to London to dance in the Music Halls and was billed as 'Madame Finette' in the *Cancan, la Danse Nationale Française*.

9. HARMONY IN GREEN AND ROSE: THE MUSIC ROOM. Canvas, 95·5×70·8 cm. Washington, Freer Gallery of Art.

Painted in 1860. The lady standing is Miss Boot: the little girl is Annie Haden, while Mrs. Haden's reflection is captured in the mirror. The room is in the Haden's house at 62 Sloane Street, London. This picture was exhibited at Goupil's in 1892. It was bought from the artist by his half-brother George W. Whistler.

10. BLACK LION WHARF. Etching. 15·2×22·6 cm. K. 42. 1859.

No. 1 of a *Series of Sixteen Etchings of Scenes on the Thames and other Subjects* (*The Thames Set*).

11. WAPPING. Canvas. 71×101 cm. Signed and dated Whistler 1861. New York, Mr. and Mrs. John Hay Whitney.

Despite the date inscribed on the canvas, this picture which caused the artist much trouble, as he explained in one of his letters to Fantin-Latour, was not finished until 1864, when it was shown at the Royal Academy. The two main figures are Jo and the French artist Alphonse Legros who taught at the South Kensington School of Art and later at the Slade School. The balcony also appears in the etching *Rotherhithe* (Plate 16).

Two sketches for this painting exist; one is on a blank page of the artist's current passport, now at Glasgow University, and the other was included in a letter to Fantin-Latour. The picture was exhibited at the Royal Academy, 1864, at the Exposition Universelle in Paris, 1867 and in Baltimore, 1876 and New York, 1878.

12. DETAIL OF PLATE II.

13. THE THAMES IN ICE. Canvas. 74·6×55·3 cm. Signed Whistler. Washington, Freer Gallery of Art.

The original title of this picture was *The Twenty-fifth of December 1860 on the Thames*. It was exhibited at the Royal Academy in 1862 and at the International Society in 1890.

14. THE LITTLE POOL. Etching. 10·3×12·5 cm. K. 74. 1861.

The man standing, Serjeant Thomas, was also a patron of Legros and Holman Hunt and brought Delâtre over to print Whistler's etchings; he was a keen judge of port wine. The man sketching is Percy Thomas and the boy Ralph Thomas. No. 10 of a *Series of Sixteen Etchings of Scenes on the Thames and other Subjects* (*The Thames Set*).

15. SOUPE À TROIS SOUS. Etching. 15·3×22·7 cm. K. 49.

This was done in Paris in about 1861 in a *cabaret* kept by Martin, who is portrayed in the print; he had won the Cross of the Legion d'Honneur and then lost it for 'some shameful deed'. (Pennell, *Life* I, p. 70.)

16. ROTHERHITHE: WAPPING. Etching. 27×19·7 cm. K. 66. 1860.

No. 5 of *A Series of Sixteen Etchings of Scenes on the Thames and other Subjects* (*The Thames Set*) under the title of 'Wapping'.

17. THE STORM. Etching. 15·5×28·4 cm. K. 81. 1861.

18. THE COAST OF BRITTANY. Canvas. 87·2×116·7 cm. Signed and dated Whistler 1861. Hartford, Conn., Wadsworth Atheneum.

When exhibited at the Royal Academy in 1862 this picture was known as *Alone with the Tide*. It was the first major picture the artist painted of the sea. He went to Brittany in the autumn of 1861. Brittany had been visited by his friend Bonvin some eight years before, and became a favourite haunt for artists. It was exhibited in Baltimore, 1876 and at the Society of American Artists, New York, 1878.

19. THE BLUE WAVE: BIARRITZ. Canvas. 62·2×6·4 cm. Signed and dated Whistler 1862. Farmington, Conn., Hill-Stead Museum.

This was painted when the artist was staying on the coast of Guéthary between Biarritz and St. Jean de Luz in the autumn of 1862 on the way to Madrid which in the event he did not visit. The motif of the breaking wave anticipates the series of seascapes which Courbet started to paint when he and Whistler were there together in 1865. In an undated letter to Fantin-Latour, from Guéthary, Whistler talks about painting *en plein air* and it would be reasonable to suppose that this picture was done 'out of doors after nature'. It was first exhibited at the Goupil Gallery in 1892.

20. BROWN AND SILVER: OLD BATTERSEA BRIDGE. Canvas, subsequently mounted on prestwood. 63·5×76·2 cm. Andover, Mass., Addison Gallery of American Art.

Commissioned by Alexander Ionides, the Anglo-Greek merchant, who was a collector of paintings and Hellenistic statuettes, and exhibited at the Royal Academy in 1865. It was also shown at the Exposition Universelle in 1867 and at Goupil's in 1892. An X-ray photograph has revealed the beginning of a self-portrait beneath the barge and the water on the right.

21. BATTERSEA REACH. Canvas. 51×76 cm. Washington, Corcoran Gallery of Art.

This picture was painted in about 1863–64. Whistler had leased 7 Lindsey Row (now 101 Cheyne Walk) early in 1863. In a letter of 17th August 1893 he described it as having been painted 'on a brilliant autumn evening'.

22. THE LAST OF OLD WESTMINSTER. Canvas. 61×77 cm. Signed and dated Whistler 1862. Boston, Museum of Fine Arts.

This was painted from the upper-floor windows of Arthur Severn's brother's rooms in Manchester Buildings (the present-day site of Scotland Yard). Severn's account, which is given by Pennell (*Life* I, pp. 100–101), indicates that the scene depicted is not the dismantling of the bridge but the removing of the scaffolding from the new one. 'He would look steadily at a pile for some time, then mix up the colour, then holding his brush quite at the end, with no mahlstick, make a downward stroke and the pile was done. I remember once his looking very carefully at a hansom cab that had pulled up for some purpose on the bridge, and in a few strokes he got the look of it perfectly. He was a long time over the picture, sometimes coming only once a week, and we got rather tired of it.' It was exhibited at the Royal Academy in 1863. It was once owned by John Carafy, a relative of the Ionides family.

23. DETAIL OF PLATE 20.

24. DETAIL OF PLATE 22.

25. SYMPHONY IN WHITE NO. 1: THE WHITE GIRL. Canvas. 214·6×108 cm. Signed and dated Whistler 1862. Washington, National Gallery of Art.

The model is Jo. This picture was rejected at the Royal Academy in 1862 but it was shown at Mathew Morgan's Gallery at 14 Berners Street, London, in the summer of the same year. It had been started in the winter of 1861. It was likewise rejected at the Salon of 1863 but shown, with immense success, at the Salon des Refusés. Thoré Burger, one of the most intelligent critics of the day, noted that this picture occasioned the greatest comment and this in an exhibition which included Manet's *Le Dejeuner sur l'Herbe* now in the Louvre.

26. ROSE AND SILVER: LA PRINCESSE DU PAYS DE LA PORCELAINE. Canvas. 199·9×116·1 cm. Signed and dated Whistler 1864. Washington, Freer Gallery of Art.

This was exhibited at the Salon of 1865, the International Exhibition at the South Kensington Museum in 1871 and at the International Society of Sculptors, Painters and Gravers in 1898 of which Whistler was the first President. The sitter is Christine Spartali, a daughter of Michael Spartali, the Greek Consul General in London and a friend of the Ionides family, and the sister of Marie Spartali who was painted by Rossetti. Christine later became Mrs. Edmond de Cahen. It was finished after innumerable sittings. A sketch for this picture, now in the Worcester Art Museum, Mass., depicts another model, whose appearance is more Japanese. The picture was later acquired by Whistler's patron, F. R. Leyland, and hung in the Peacock Room at Princes Gate, London.

27. SLEEPING WOMAN–STUDY FOR THE ETCHING 'WEARY'. Black Crayon Drawing. 25·5×17·6 cm. Signed Whistler. Washington, National Gallery of Art, Rosenwald Collection

The model is Jo. The etching (K. 92) was exhibited at the Royal Academy in 1863. Another study for 'Weary' is the Clark Art Institute, Williamstown, Mass.: See *Catalogue*, 1964 (no. 355).

28. PURPLE AND ROSE: THE LANGE LIJZEN OF THE SIX MARKS. Canvas. 91×56 cm. Signed and dated Whistler 1864. Philadelphia, Museum of Art, John G. Johnson Collection.

The frame which has oriental motives was specially designed for the picture. The porcelain and carpet shown in the picture belonged to the artist. The title refers to the Delft term for the decorative figures on the jar in the picture: 'Of the six marks' refers to the signature and date found on rare china of this type. It was exhibited at the Royal Academy in 1864, at Newcastle three years later and at Goupil's in 1892.

29. DETAIL OF PLATE 25.

30. CAPRICE IN PURPLE AND GOLD NO. 2: THE GOLDEN SCREEN. Panel. 50×68·5 cm. Signed and dated Whistler 1864. Washington, Freer Gallery of Art.

It was exhibited at the Royal Academy in 1865. The sitter is Jo and the prints on the screen and the floor are by Hiroshige.

31. DETAIL OF PLATE 30.

32. DETAIL OF FRONTISPIECE.

33. HARMONY IN BLUE AND SILVER: TROUVILLE. Canvas. 50×76 cm. Boston, Isabella Stewart Gardner Museum.

The butterfly signature was added in 1892 at the request of the famous Bostonian collector Mrs. J. L. Gardner when she bought it from the artist in Paris in that year. The figure in the foreground is Courbet. It was painted between August and September 1865 when Whistler was in Trouville with this painter. Jo was also there and on this occasion Courbet painted her as 'La Belle Irlandaise'.

34. HARMONY IN GREY: CHELSEA IN ICE. Canvas. 44·7×61 cm. London, Private Collection.

This picture was bought from the artist by Mme. Emilie Venturi, the friend of Mazzini. It was probably exhibited at the Sixth Exhibition of the Society of French Artists, London, 1873. It was exhibited at the R.B.A. in 1887 and at Goupil's in 1892. It is possibly one of the two pictures which the artist's mother mentioned in a letter of 10th February 1864 as her son having painted from the windows of Lindsey House. 'During a very sharp frost of a few days, I think for two days, ice was passing as we looked out upon the Thames. He could not resist painting, while I was shivering at the open window, two sketches which all say are most effective; one takes in the bridge. Of course, they are not finished; he could not leave his Oriental pictures.' (*Atlantic Monthly*, CXXVI, 1925, pp. 318–28). Mr. McLaren Young is inclined to date the painting rather later.

35. CREPUSCULE IN FLESH COLOUR AND GREEN: VALPARAISO. Canvas. 57·2×75·5 cm. Signed and dated Whistler. Valparaiso. 1866. London, Tate Gallery.

The artist went to South America in February 1866 and returned to London in November of the same year. The precise reasons for this journey have never been explained. He seems to have spent much of his time in Valparaiso and while there the country was undergoing one of its many revolutions. He painted in this city, or, at any rate, worked out the ideas for about half a dozen landscapes. First exhibited at the French Gallery, London, in 1867, and later at the Paris Salon of 1891, at Goupil's in 1892, and at the International Exhibition at Venice in 1899. It was originally owned by C. A. Howell and at his sale at Christie's in November 1890 it was acquired by the artist, writer and collector W. Graham Robertson who also bought No. 71 in the same sale.

36. SYMPHONY IN GREY AND GREEN: THE OCEAN. Canvas. 79·5×99 cm. Butterfly signature. New York, Frick Collection.

Painted either during or as a result of the artist's visit to South America in 1866. It was exhibited in the Exposition Universelle, Paris, 1867, Dudley Gallery 1872, at the Paris Salon of 1892, the Grosvenor Gallery 1879 and at Goupil's in 1892.

37. NOCTURNE IN BLUE AND GOLD: VALPARAISO. Canvas. 75·6×50·1 cm. Washington, Freer Gallery of Art.

This picture, which was exhibited at the Society of British Artists in 1887, once belonged to Henry Hill, the Brighton collector who owned several important pictures by Degas and was bought at his sale of 1889 by Alexander Ionides. An oil study for this picture is reproduced by Pennell (*Life*, I, facing page 134). Exhibited at Goupil's in 1892 and at the International Society in 1898.

38. DESIGN FOR A MOSAIC. Pastel on brown paper. 28×17·5 cm. Butterfly signature. Private Collection.

This drawing, sometimes called the Gold Girl, is the preliminary sketch for a decorative scheme which in 1873 Sir Henry Cole, the Director of the South Kensington Museum (now the Victoria and Albert Museum), invited the artist to undertake for the central gallery of the museum. Although a cartoon was prepared in a studio which was made available to the artist in the museum, the decoration was never carried out.

39. 'ANNABEL LEE'. Pastel. 32·3×18 cm. Butterfly signature. 1860's. Washington, Freer Gallery of Art.

This work was formerly called *Niobe* but since the London memorial exhibition of 1905, it has been known as *Annabel Lee*. In the 1860's Whistler began work on a painting inspired by Poe's poem with the title. It was seen in the early stages by William Graham, the art-loving Scottish M.P. and a patron of the Pre-Raphaelites, who paid for it. However, the composition did not please the artist and the picture exists in a rubbed down condition in Glasgow University. There is an oil sketch as well as a number of drawings connected with the composition in this collection. A pen and ink sketch, which is a variant of the Glasgow picture, is reproduced by Pennell, *Life*, II, p. 316.

40. SYMPHONY IN WHITE NO. 3. Canvas. 52×76·5 cm. Inscribed, signed and dated *Symphony in White No. III. Whistler 1867*. The figure 7 is written over the figure 5. Birmingham, Barber Institute of Fine Arts.

The girls on the sofa are Jo Heffernan and Milly Jones, who was married to an actor called Robson. In one of his letters to Fantin-Latour the artist discussed this picture at length, including a sketch of it, and ventilating his conception of anti-realism. It shows his close connections with the artist Albert Moore at this date. This is the first of Whistler's pictures to be given a musical title. It once belonged to Louis Huth who, like the artist, was an admirer of Velasquez. Mrs. Huth was painted by Whistler in 1863 (see note on Plate 75). It was exhibited at the Royal Academy, 1867, Society of French Artists, London, 1873, the Société des XX, Brussels, 1884, and at Goupil's in 1892. A copy of this picture by Degas appears in a sketch book of 1865–68 in the Louvre. It is based on the sketch sent by Whistler to Fantin-Latour.

41. THREE FIGURES: PINK AND GREY. Canvas. 144·8×185·4 cm. London, Tate Gallery.

This was apparently painted in the winter of 1867–68 when the artist was sharing rooms with Frederick Jameson at 62 Great Russell Street. He was tempted to paint another *Symphony in White* which would be no. 4. Besides this picture there is an oil sketch forming one of the Six Projects in the Freer Gallery, Washington and a number of drawings in the Birnie Philip Bequest, Glasgow. The project seems to have connected with the picture which, according to W. M. Rossetti, he was painting for F. R. Leyland in 1867: see Pennell, *Life*, I, p. 149. The Tate Gallery picture, which was with Dowdeswell's in 1891, subsequently belonged to Alfred Chapman and then to the Princess de Polignac, whose Paris *salon* was described by Marcel Proust.

42. SYMPHONY IN BLUE AND PINK. Prepared Academy Board mounted on Panel. 46·7×61·9 cm. About 1868. Washington, Freer Gallery of Art.

One of the 'Six Projects'.

43. VARIATIONS IN BLUE AND GREEN. Prepared Academy Board mounted on panel. 46·9×61·8 cm. Washington, Freer Gallery of Art.

One of the 'Six Projects'.

44. VARIATIONS IN FLESH COLOUR AND GREEN: THE BALCONY. Panel. 61·4×48·8 cm. About 1867–68. Washington, Freer Gallery of Art.

The artist was anxious to produce a life-size picture of this composition for the Salon, but this was never done. The oil sketch in the University of Glasgow which reveals traces of alteration and is squared for possible enlargement may be connected with the project. Although the scene is Oriental, the background is of the Thames.

45. THE ARTIST'S STUDIO. Panel. 62·9×47·6 cm. Chicago, Art Institute.

The artist was working on a large-scale picture on this theme in 1867–68 which may have been inspired by Fantin-Latour's *Hommage à la Verité: Le Toast* in which he himself was represented; this work was subsequently dismembered, although the portrait of Whistler survives and is now in the Freer Gallery, Washington. Whistler made two sketches for this picture; both, in addition to the artist himself, show Jo and a model known as 'La Japonaise'. The other sketch is in the Municipal Art Gallery, Dublin.

46. DETAIL OF PLATE 44.

47. DETAIL OF PLATE 40.

48. TWO FEMALE FIGURES. Chalk drawing. 20·6×18·1 cm. About 1868. Cambridge, Mass., Fogg Art Museum.

49. VENUS RISING FROM THE SEA. Canvas. 61·9×45·6 cm. About 1868. Washington, Freer Gallery of Art.

50. SPEKE HALL. Etching. 22·5×15 cm. K. 96. 1870.

51. VARIATIONS IN VIOLET AND GREEN. Canvas. 61×35·5 cm. Butterfly signature and dated 1871. U.S.A., Private Collection.

Exhibited at the Dudley Gallery in 1871. This important picture looks ahead to the Nocturnes and the other Thames pictures of the 1870's. The frame, designed and decorated by Whistler is also signed with a butterfly and dated 1871.

52. A GIRL READING. Black crayon on brown paper. 27·9×18·1 cm. Butterfly signature. Glasgow University, Birnie Philip Gift.

53. ARRANGEMENT IN GREY AND BLACK NO. I: THE ARTIST'S MOTHER. Canvas. 145×164 cm. Butterfly signature. Paris, Louvre.

First exhibited at the Royal Academy in 1872 and later at Philadelphia, 1881, the Salon, 1883 and at Amsterdam, 1889. It was acquired by the French State in 1891 with the support of a number of leading French artists; it may well have exerted some influence over Toulouse-Lautrec's *Portrait of Paul Leclercq* in the Louvre (Fig. 11). The print on the left of the composition is the artist's Black Lion Wharf (No. 10). It has been suggested by John Sandberg, 'Japonisme and Whistler' in *Burlington Magazine*, CVI, November, 1964, pp. 500–507, that the picture of his mother referred to by Whistler in a letter, apparently dating from 1867, to Fantin-Latour may be identical with this work and that it was painted over a five year period.

54. DETAIL OF PLATE 57.

55. DETAIL OF PLATE 53.

56. HARMONY IN GREY AND GREEN: MISS CICELY ALEXANDER. Canvas. 218·4×99 cm. Butterfly signature. London, Tate Gallery.

This celebrated picture, which indicates the artist's debt to Velasquez, was painted in seventy sittings in 1873 and exhibited at the artist's show at 48 Pall Mall in the following year. The sitter, later Mrs. Bernard Spring-Rice (1864–1932) was the second daughter of W. C. Alexander, the patron of the artist and a collector of Blue and White Porcelain. The artist supervised her clothes for this portrait and even directed where the gown was to be laundered. The sitter herself wrote to the Pennells, *Life*, I, p. 174: 'I was painted at the little house in Chelsea, and at the time he was decorating the staircase . . . the studio was at the back of the house and the drawing room looked over the river, and we seldom went into it but I remember that it had matting on the floor, and a large Japanese basin with water, and a goldfish in it.' An oil sketch of the girl's head is in Mrs. J.

Hampden Robb's collection, Beverly Farm, Mass. A full-length pastel for, or connected with, the picture is in Miss Alexander's collection, London, and a drawing is reproduced by Duret, p. 36.

57. ARRANGEMENT IN GREY AND BLACK NO. 2: THOMAS CARLYLE. Canvas. 171 × 143·5 cm. Butterfly signature. Glasgow, City Art Gallery and Museum.

Sittings started for this portrait in 1872 and were still going on in the July of the following year. An oil study of the head and shoulders is in Haverford College, Pennsylvania, and a pen and ink sketch connected with the portrait is illustrated in Pennell, *Life*, I, facing page 170. This picture which has been much exhibited was first shown at the artist's show at 48, Pall Mall, London, in 1874, and then at the Grosvenor Gallery in 1877. It was acquired by the Corporation of Glasgow in 1891.

58. DETAIL OF PLATE 56.

59. ARRANGEMENT IN GREY: SELF-PORTRAIT. Canvas. 74·9 × 53·3 cm. Butterfly signature. Detroit, Institute of Arts.

Painted between 1871 and 1873, in which year it was shown at the Society of French Artists' 6th Exhibition. Ten years later it was exhibited at the Exposition Internationale at the Galerie Georges Petit, Paris and at Goupil's in 1895. It was bought from the artist by Alexander Ionides and etched by Percy Thomas as the frontispiece to *A Catalogue of the Etchings and Drypoints of James Abbott McNeill Whistler in 1874*.

60. ARRANGEMENT IN BLACK: PORTRAIT OF F. R. LEYLAND. Canvas. 192·8 × 91·9 cm. Butterfly signature. Washington, Freer Gallery of Art.

This portrait of F. R. Leyland, the owner of the Leyland Shipping Line, a collector, accomplished musician and patron of the artist, was finished by the winter of 1873 and exhibited at the Pall Mall exhibition in the following year. An oil sketch belonged to Charles Conder and is illustrated in Pennell, *Life*, I, p. 178. According to Pennell, *Life*, I, p. 176, 'Leyland was good about standing, Mrs. Leyland says, but he had not much time, and few portraits gave Whistler more trouble. Leyland told Val Prinsep that Whistler nearly cried over the drawing of the legs. Mr. Greaves says that "he got into an awful mess over it", painted it out and out again, and finally had in a model to pose for it nude.'

61. SYMPHONY IN FLESH COLOUR AND PINK: MRS. F. R. LEYLAND. Canvas. 189·5 × 96 cm. Butterfly signature. New York, Frick Collection.

Painted in 1873 and exhibited in the following year at the Pall Mall exhibition. Mrs. Leyland, to whom the artist was deeply attached, had wonderful red hair and had already sat to Dante Gabriel Rossetti. Whistler also made a drypoint of her, *The Velvet Gown*. According to Pennell, *Life*, I, p. 177, she had wished to be painted in black velvet 'but he preferred a dress in harmony with her hair, and designed soft draperies of rose and white falling in sweeping folds, and rosettes of a deeper shade to break the simplicity of the flowing lines, and he placed her against a rose-tinted wall, with a spray of almond blossoms at her side.' He made a number of pastel studies of her before he decided upon the pose.

62. ARRANGEMENT IN BLACK AND WHITE: THE YOUNG AMERICAN. Canvas. 191·4 × 90 cm. Butterfly signature. Washington, Freer Gallery of Art.

First exhibited at the Grosvenor Gallery in 1874. The sitter is Maud Franklin, who became Whistler's mistress in the 1870's and was known as 'Mrs. Whistler'. She accompanied the artist to Venice in 1879–80 and remained in command until he married Beatrix Godwin. She sat for numerous paintings (cf. No. 72) and etchings.

63. THE WHITE GIRL NO. 4. Canvas. 194·3 × 99·7 cm. Butterfly signature. Cambridge, Mass., Fogg Art Museum.

Painted around 1872–1874. It was shown at the Pall Mall exhibition in 1874.

64. NOCTURNE IN BLUE AND SILVER: CREMORNE LIGHTS. Canvas. 49·5 × 74 cm. Butterfly signature and dated 72. London, Tate Gallery.

Probably first shown at the Winter Exhibition at the Dudley Gallery in 1872; later it was exhibited at the Grosvenor Gallery in 1882 and at Goupil's in 1892. This is one of the artist's early Nocturnes. It was owned by the painter Arthur Studd in the 1890's.

65. NOCTURNE IN BLUE AND GREEN: CHELSEA. Panel. 48·2 × 39·8 cm. Signed with butterfly. London, Miss J. Alexander.

This picture, which seems to be the earliest of the Thames Nocturnes painted by the artist in the 1870's was bought by W. C. Alexander, the collector and patron in 1871 or 1872. It was exhibited at the Dudley Gallery in 1871 under the title 'Harmony in Blue-green – Moonlight' and at the Grosvenor Gallery in 1879. It was probably shown at the Société des XX in Brussels in 1884. It was exhibited at Goupil's in 1892, and at the Burlington Fine Arts Club in 1903. Until F. R. Leyland suggested the name Nocturne for such pictures, Whistler used to call them 'Moonlights'.

66. NOCTURNE IN BLUE AND GOLD: OLD BATTERSEA BRIDGE. Canvas. 66·6×50·2 cm. London, Tate Gallery.

It probably dates from about 1872–75 and was given to the Glasgow collector William Graham, M.P. in lieu of *Annabel Lee* (see Plate 39) which he had paid for but which the artist never finished. It was originally entitled *Nocturne in Blue and Silver, No. 5*, but it was re-named by Whistler when shown at Goupil's in 1892. It was first exhibited at the Grosvenor Gallery in 1877.

67. NOCTURNE IN BLACK AND GOLD: THE FIRE WHEEL. Canvas. 53·5×75·5 cm. London, Tate Gallery.

Painted in about 1874–75. The artist made a preliminary study in pen and ink and a watercolour copy of the picture which is now in Glasgow University. First exhibited at the Grosvenor Gallery in 1883 and later at the Paris Salon of 1888 as well as at Munich, 1888 and New York, 1889.

68. CREMORNE GARDENS NO. 2. Canvas. 68·5×135·5 cm. New York, Metropolitan Museum of Art.

Painted in about 1875. Cremorne Gardens by the Thames in Chelsea was a popular resort which closed down in 1877. The artist painted other pictures of the same place; they were all distinguished by their technical daring.

69. DETAIL OF PLATE 68.

70. NOCTURNE IN BLACK AND GOLD: THE FALLING ROCKET. Panel. 60·3×46·6 cm. Detroit, Institute of Art.

Painted in about 1874. It was this picture, more than any other work by the artist, which gave rise to Ruskin's attack on Whistler in *Fors Clavigera*. This in turn led to the celebrated law case between Ruskin and Whistler. First exhibited at the Dudley Gallery in 1875 and then at the Grosvenor Gallery in 1877. It was shown in New York in 1889 and at Goupil's in 1892.

71. ARRANGEMENT IN BLACK AND BROWN: ROSA CORDER. Canvas. 190·8×89·8 cm. New York, Frick Collection.

Rosa Corder was an intimate friend of C. A. Howell, who apparently commissioned this portrait. It was painted in the 1870's and exhibited at the Grosvenor Gallery in 1879, at the Salon in 1891, at Goupil's in 1892 and at the International Society of Painters, Gravers and Sculptors in 1898. A pen and ink sketch was once in the collection of Alan S. Cole and is reproduced in Pennell, *Life*, I, p. 296, and an oil study of her head is reproduced in *Art in America*, July 1939, p. 136. The sitter studied under Felix Moscheles and painted race horses. She is alleged to have assisted Howell in copying old paintings and drawings. This portrait as well as the *Crepuscule in Flesh Colour and Green: Valparaiso* (Plate 35) were acquired by the painter W. Graham Robertson at the Howell sale at Christie's in November, 1890. Whistler wrote to Robertson asking if he could 'see them hanging on your walls' expressing the wish to meet 'the collector who so far ventures to brave popular prejudice in this country.' Whistler told Robertson that he believed the portrait of Rosa Corder was 'the only thing he ever paid for in his life: I was amazed when I got the cheque, and I only remembered some months afterwards that he had paid me out of my own money which I had lent to him the week before'. Robertson recounts in his memoirs *Time Was* (1931) that Rosa Corder told him that she had posed some forty times 'standing in a doorway with the darkness of a shuttered room beyond her; long sittings, lasting on two occasions until she fainted, and at last she had refused to go on with them'.

72. ARRANGEMENT IN BLACK AND BROWN: THE FUR JACKET. Canvas. 194×92·7 cm. Butterfly signature. Worcester, Mass., Art Museum.

Painted in the 1870's. First exhibited at the Grosvenor Gallery in 1877, it was shown at Amsterdam two years later, and at Goupil's in 1892. The model is Maud Franklin.

73. HARMONY IN YELLOW AND GOLD: THE GOLD GIRL, CONNIE GILCHRIST. Canvas. 217×109·5 cm. Butterfly signature and inscribed *Connie Gilchrist*. New York, Metropolitan Museum of Art.

Painted in about 1876 and exhibited at the Grosvenor Gallery in 1879. It appeared in the artist's bankruptcy sale at Sotheby's in 1880. Connie Gilchrist (1865–1946) appeared at the Gaiety Theatre as a skipping-rope dancer; in the late 80's she married the Earl of Orkney. A pen and ink sketch of her is in the British Museum; another oil portrait is at Glasgow University.

74. ARRANGEMENT IN YELLOW AND GREY: EFFIE DEANS. Canvas. 194×93 cm. Amsterdam, Rijksmuseum.

Butterfly signature and inscribed . . .

> she sunk her head upon her hand
> and remained seemingly
> unconscious as a statue
> The Heart of Midlothian
> Walter Scott.

Painted in 1876, the model is almost certainly Maud Franklin. It was exhibited at the International Exhibition of 1888 at Edinburgh and bought, at around this date, by the Dutch dealer E. J. van Wisselingh, who sold it to a Dutch collector Baron van Lynden. The butterfly was added in about 1889 by the artist at the owner's request. The inscription is also later. It is one of the three pictures with a literary theme which Whistler painted; the other two are the unfinished *Annabel Lee* and *Ariel.*

75. STUDY FOR THE PORTRAIT OF MRS. LOUIS HUTH. Pastel. 26·4×16·5 cm. Oxford, Ashmolean Museum.

Whistler's portrait of Mrs. Huth was bought for 600 guineas by the sitter's husband early in 1873 and now belongs to Viscount Cowdray.

76. ARRANGEMENT IN BLACK NO. 3: SIR HENRY IRVING IN THE CHARACTER OF PHILIP II OF SPAIN IN TENNYSON'S 'QUEEN MARY'. Canvas. 215 ×108·6 cm. New York, Metropolitan Museum of Art.

Although exhibited at the Grosvenor Gallery in 1877, the artist did not consider that the picture was satisfactorily finished and seems to have persuaded the famous actor to pose for him again in about 1885. Two sketchy etchings of the same sitter seem to relate to the early state of the picture. It was bought from the artist by C. A. Howell for 'ten Pounds and a seal-skin coat' in 1878 and shown in the Salon of 1880. Before 1885 it was acquired by Irving. It was also exhibited at the London Whistler exhibition of 1889 and the Grafton Gallery in 1897 and at Edinburgh 1904.

77. NOCTURNE IN BLUE AND SILVER: BATTERSEA REACH. Canvas. 39×63 cm. Boston, Isabella Stewart Gardner Museum.

Painted in the 1870's and bought by Mrs. J. L. Gardner from the artist in 1895 and exhibited in March 1898 at the Copley and Alston Halls as 'Symphony in blue'.

78. NOCTURNE IN BROWN AND GOLD: CHELSEA RAGS. Canvas. 36·2×50·8 cm. Cambridge, Mass., Fogg Art Museum.

Painted in about 1878 and exhibited at Dowdeswell's in 1884 and at the International Society in 1899.

79. NOCTURNE: WESTMINSTER PALACE. Canvas. 31·12×51·43 cm. Philadelphia, Museum of Art, John G. Johnson Collection.

Painted in the late 1870's This belonged to Théodore Duret and while in his collection was described by George Moore in *Modern Painting*, 1893, pp. 22–23. 'Mr. Whistler's nights are the blue transparent darknesses which are half of the world's life. Sometimes he foregoes even the aid of earthly light, and his picture is but luminous blue shadow, delicately graduated, as in the nocturne in M. Duret's collection – purple above and below, a shadow in the middle of the picture – a little less and there would be nothing.'

80. NOCTURNE IN GREY AND GOLD: CHELSEA SNOW. Canvas. 44·5×61 cm. Cambridge, Mass., Fogg Art Museum.

First exhibited at the Grosvenor Gallery in 1878 and then at Goupil's in 1892.

81. NOCTURNE: CREMORNE GARDENS, NO. 3. Canvas. 44·9×63·1 cm. Washington, Freer Gallery of Art.

Painted between 1875–77. This once belonged to Charles Conder.

82. GREY AND SILVER: THE ANGRY SEA. Panel. 12·4 ×21·7 cm. Butterfly signature. Washington, Freer Gallery of Art.

Exhibited at Dowdeswell's in 1884.

83. NOCTURNE IN BLACK AND GOLD: ENTRANCE TO SOUTHAMPTON WATERS. Canvas. 50·9×76·3 cm. Butterfly signature. Chicago, Art Institute.

Painted in the late 1870's or early 1880's and first exhibited at the Grosvenor Gallery in 1884 and then at Goupil's in 1892.

84. NOCTURNE IN BLUE AND SILVER: THE LAGOON, VENICE. Canvas. 51×66 cm. Boston, Museum of Fine Arts.

The artist arrived in Venice in 1879 and remained there until 1880. He painted a few oil pictures but most of his time was spent making etchings and pastels. This work was stolen by Carmen Rossi with a number of other pictures from the artist's Paris studio.

85. THE MAST. Etching. 34×16 cm. K. 195. No. 10 of Second Series. Published in 1886.

During his year in Venice the artist made many etchings; he had arrived in the city with a specific commission from the Fine Art Society to undertake a series of twelve etched plates. In all he made about forty prints, of which twelve were published in 1880, immediately on his return – *The First Set*, and the remainder set of twenty-seven in 1888. He made clear his method in such prints to his pupil Mortimer Menpes: 'I began first of all by seizing upon the chief points of interest. Perhaps it might have been the extreme distance – the little palaces and the shipping beneath the bridge. If so, I would begin drawing that distance in elaborately, and then would expand from it, until I came to the bridge, which I would draw in one broad sweep. If by chance I did not see the whole of the bridge, I would not put it in. In this way, the picture must necessarily be a perfect thing from start to finish. Even if one were to be arrested in the middle of it, it would still be a fine and complete picture.'

86. ALLEY IN VENICE. Pastel. 26 × 17·8 cm. Butterfly signature. Cambridge, Mass., Fogg Art Museum.

During his time in Venice, the artist made many delightful pastels. The Pennells pointed out that 'There were two reasons why Whistler used coloured papers for the pastels. One was that they gave him, without any work at all, the foundation of a colour scheme which could be carried out in the simplest manner in the black chalk outline, and the few touches of pastel that completed the harmony. The other reason was that, having the sympathetic colour of the paper, he worked straightaway on it, and did not ruin the surface and tire himself in getting the tone.' *Life*, I, p. 277. Fifty-three pastels were exhibited at the Fine Art Society in 1881. Godwin gave a description of the gallery, which has been specially designed by the artist, in the *British Architect* (February, 1881): 'First, a low skirting of yellow gold, then a high dado of dull yellow green cloth, then a moulding of green gold, and then a frieze and ceiling of pale reddish brown. The frames are arranged on the line; but here and there one is placed over another. Most of the frames and mounts are of rich yellow gold, but a dozen out of the fifty-three are in green gold, dotted about with a view of decoration and eminently successful in attaining it.' The exhibition was a success.

87. THE BALCONY. Etching from the *Second Set*. 29·5 × 20 cm. K. 207. Published in 1880.

88. NOCTURNE: PALACES. Etching. 29 × 20 cm. K. 202. Published in the set of *Venice, Second Series*.

89. RIVA DEGLI SCHIAVONI AT SUNSET. Pastel. 18·4 × 27·9 cm. Butterfly signature. Cambridge, Mass., Fogg Art Museum.

90. STORMY SUNSET. Pastel. 18·4 × 50·8 cm. Butterfly signature. Cambridge, Mass., Fogg Art Museum.

Possibly No. 28 in the exhibition at the Fine Art Society, 1881.

91. HARMONY IN FLESH COLOUR AND PINK: LADY MEUX. Canvas. 190·5 × 90·5 cm. Butterfly signature. New York, Frick Collection.

First exhibited at the Grosvenor Gallery in 1882, then at Dublin in 1884, at the Salon of 1892 and at Goupil's in 1892. The second of the three portraits which the artist painted of the wife of H. B. Meux, the brewer, later Sir Henry Meux, in 1881. The first of these is in the collection of Mr. Ian Gilmour and the third, showing her in furs and with a muff, was destroyed.

92. ARRANGEMENT IN FLESH COLOUR AND BLACK: PORTRAIT OF THÉODORE DURET. Canvas. 194 × 90·8 cm. Butterfly signature. New York, Metropolitan Museum of Art.

The well-known French art critic, Duret, was a defender of the French Impressionists and the author of a volume on Whistler in which he left an account of the methods employed by the artist in painting the portrait in 1882–84. It was first exhibited in the Salon of 1885.

93. ARRANGEMENT IN BLACK: LADY IN A YELLOW BUSKIN – LADY ARCHIBALD CAMPBELL. Canvas. 213 × 109 cm. Philadelphia, Museum of Art, Wilstach Collection.

First exhibited at the Grosvenor Gallery in 1884 and later at the Salon, 1885 and at Munich, 1888. Lady Archibald, who first sat for her portrait in 1883, was married to the second son of the eighth Duke of Argyll and was herself keenly interested in art and interior decoration.

She told the Pennells (*Life*, I, p. 305): 'I think I sat to him during a year or so, off and on, for a very great many studies in different costumes and poses. His first idea was to paint me in court dress. The dress was black velvet, the train was silver satin with the Argyll arms embroidered in *appliqué* in their proper colours. He made a sketch of me in this dress. The fatigue of standing with the train was too great, and he abandoned the idea. In all these studies I remember he called my attention to his method of placing his subject well within the frame, and explaining that a portrait must be more than a portrait, must be of value decoratively, that is to say, it must be decorative in purpose. He never patched up defects, but if with any portion of his work he became dissatisfied, he covered the canvas over afresh with his first impression freshly recorded. The first impression thrown on the canvas he often put away, often destroyed. Among others, he made in oil colour an impression of me as Orlando, in the forest scene of *As You Like It*, at Coombe. He considered this successful. A picture which he called *The Grey Lady* was a harmony in silver greys. I remember thinking it was a masterpiece of drawing, giving the impression of movement. I was descending the steps of a stair, the canvas was of a great height and the general effect very striking. That picture was almost completed, when my absence from town prevented a continuance of the sittings. When I returned, he asked to make a study of me in the dress in which I called upon him. This is the picture which he exhibited under the name of *The Brodequin Jaune*, or *The Yellow Buskin*. I understand it is now at Philadelphia. As far as I remember it was painted in a very few sittings. When I saw him very shortly before his death, I remember asking after *The Grey Lady*. He laughed, and said he had destroyed her.' Pennell also supplied an account of the exchanges between the sitter and the artist which ended in the latter's discouragement.

94. ROSE AND SILVER: PORTRAIT OF MRS. CHARLES WHIBLEY. Watercolour. 22·8×18·8 cm. Butterfly signature. Washington, Freer Gallery of Art.

Mrs. Charles Whibley was Ethel Philip, the sister of Beatrix Philip, the artist's wife. She had married Charles Whibley, the well-known journalist and man of letters and a friend and associate of W. E. Henley, in 1895. They were married in Paris from Whistler's house in the Rue du Bac. He also painted her as *L'Andalouse* (Glasgow University) in about 1894. Whistler designed a cover for Whibley's *A Book of Scoundrels* published by his friend William Heinemann in 1897.

95. ARRANGEMENT IN BLACK: PABLO DE SARASATE. Canvas. 217×111·7 cm. Butterfly signature. Pittsburgh, Carnegie Institute.

This picture of the famous violinist Pablo de Sarasate y Navacues (1844–1908) was finished by July 1884 and exhibited at the Society of British Artists, London, in 1885, at the Paris Salon of 1886 and at the Société des XX in Brussels in the same year. It was acquired by the Carnegie Institute, Pittsburgh, in 1897. A pen and ink sketch is reproduced by Pennell, *Life*, II, opp. p. 4.

96. HARMONY IN RED: LAMPLIGHT – MRS. WHISTLER. Canvas. 188×89 cm. Butterfly signature. Glasgow University, Birnie Philip Gift.

Beatrix (Trixie) was the daughter of John Birnie Philip, the sculptor, and was first married to J. W. Godwin, the architect and designer. She mixed in artistic circles before her marriage to Godwin and was something of an artist herself. She was a close friend of Whistler before her husband's death and married him in 1886; this portrait is painted in the same year and exhibited at the Society of British Artists in 1886. Her premature death in 1896 left the artist disconsolate.

97. GREEN AND VIOLET: MRS. WALTER SICKERT. Canvas. 86·4×61 cm. Butterfly signature. Cambridge, Mass., Fogg Art Museum.

Ellen Cobden Sickert sat to the artist in 1885 after her husband had commissioned portraits of her and himself after their marriage. This portrait was shown at the Society of British Artists in 1887. The present picture is another and later version which was first shown at the Salon in 1895. It was also probably exhibited at the Glasgow Fine Art Institute, 1895 (1) as 'Mrs. Bernard Sickert'.

98. PORTRAIT OF GEORGE A. LUCAS. Panel. 21·75×12·54 cm. Baltimore, Walters Art Gallery.

George A. Lucas knew Whistler from the early Paris days. He came from Baltimore and went to Paris in 1857, remaining there for the rest of his life. He acted as an agent for the railroad magnate William T. Walters and introduced him to Barye. He became the friend of countless artists, kept a valuable diary and formed a large collection of prints and paintings which are now in the possession of the Maryland Institute. Although he owned a number of Whistler's etchings he did not buy any of his paintings. This portrait was started on a visit to Lucas's country house in 1886 but left unfinished after two sittings. As the Pennells noted in the *Whistler Journal*, p. 56, 'It is a small portrait – anticipating the Holloway, Hannay, Kennedy, Crockett portraits'. Lucas received a number of letters from the artist, mostly dating from the early 1860's to the mid 1880's. As Miss Gertrud Rosenthal has pointed out (*The George A. Lucas Collection*, 1965): 'Whistler often asked Lucas for favors – to look after the hanging of his paintings in an exhibition and to ship them back to him in London, to have frames made, to find a studio for him preferably near to Lucas' residence. There are even delicate requests such as helping him to soothe his mistress by mailing Whistler's letters to her from Paris, while Whistler was obviously off for a pleasant rendezvous somewhere else.' Whistler also asked him to put up Maud in his apartment and he liked her so much that he invited her to stay again. It is even rumoured that because of Whistler's break with his mistress, when he married, relations between the two men became strained. In any event, Lucas always treasured Whistler's gift of Maud reading in bed. 'This', he told the Pennells, 'for the lover of Whistler is perfect.'

99. MAUD READING IN BED. Watercolour. 25×17·5 cm. Baltimore, Walters Art Gallery.

Inscribed: This Aquarelle painted by Whistler from his model Maud was presented to me by him, G. A. Lucas. Paris, France. This watercolour probably dates from the same time as Whistler's portrait of Lucas.

100. THE GOLD RUFF. 25·8×18 cm. Glasgow University, Birnie Philip Gift.

This picture may be compared with *Red and Pink – La Petite Mephisto*, which was exhibited at Dowdeswell's in 1884 (51).

101. GOLD AND ORANGE: THE NEIGHBOURS. Panel. 21·6 × 12·8 cm. Butterfly signature. Washington, Freer Gallery of Art.

Painted in the 1880's and first exhibited at the International Society in 1901.

102. UNE PETITE BONNE À LA PORTE D'UNE AUBERGE. Panel. 21·5 × 12·6 cm. Butterfly signature. New Orleans, Mr. and Mrs. Charles C. Henderson.

Painted presumably in France in the late 1890's and first exhibited at the Memorial exhibition of 1905.

103. CHELSEA SHOPS. Panel. 13·5 × 23·4 cm. Washington, Freer Gallery of Art.

One of the small oil studies which the artist painted in the early 1880's and of which a number appeared at the Dowdeswell exhibition of 1884. Mortimer Menpes has described how he and Whistler would set out for a morning's work in London. 'Then Whistler would get his little pochade box, and together we would drift out into the open – on to the Embankment, or down a side street in Chelsea – and he would make a little subject, sometimes in water, sometimes in oil colour. It might be a fish shop with eels for sale at so much a plate, and a few soiled children in the foreground; or perhaps a sweet-stuff shop, and the children standing with their faces glued to the pane. There we would stay and paint until luncheon time, sitting on rush-bottomed chairs borrowed from the nearest shop. Wherever Whistler went he caused interest and excitement: men, women and children flocked about him – especially children, Chelsea children, shoals of them.' *Whistler as I knew Him*, 1904, pp. 3–4.

104. A NOTE IN RED. Panel. 13·4 × 23·5 cm. Washington, Freer Gallery of Art.

105. SOUTHEND PIER. Watercolour. 18·2 × 25·7 cm. Butterfly signature. Washington, Freer Gallery of Art.

This is possibly identical with the *Grey and Silver – Pier, Southend*, exhibited at Dowdeswell in 1884 (62).

106. RANELAGH GARDENS. Watercolour. 12·7 × 21·9 cm. Painted in the 1880's or 1890's. Washington, Freer Gallery of Art.

107. THE STEPS – LUXEMBOURG GARDENS. Lithograph. 21 × 15·7 cm. W. 43. 1894.

108. THE EMBROIDERED CURTAIN. Etching. 23·9 × 16 cm. K. 410.

One of the group of brilliant etchings executed on the artist's visit to Holland in 1889.

109. THE GREENGROCER'S SHOP. Panel. 23·4 × 14 cm. Glasgow University, Birnie Philip Gift.

This unfinished study is one of the small oils painted by the artist in Paris during 1893–95 which recall his small Chelsea pictures.

110. DORSETSHIRE LANDSCAPE. Canvas. 32 × 62·8 cm. Butterfly signature. Washington, Freer Gallery of Art.

This was painted at Lyme Regis, where Whistler spent the summer of 1895. The late J. W. Reveillon believed that this picture is the one referred to in a letter written by Whistler to his sister-in-law Miss Birnie Philip from Paris: 'suppose you were to pack up and send to me the little sketch of skys and tops of houses that hangs in the bedroom upstairs. I could sign and look at it and see if it may be worth mounting in a proper frame'. In a second letter he said 'enclosed I send cheque for two hundred guineas for the little picture of Devonshire cottages that you have had hanging in desperate loneliness at the top of the house for all these years.' If this letter does refer to this picture, Devonshire would be a slip for Dorsetshire. The painting was once in the possession of Alexander Young who lent it to the memorial exhibition of 1905.

111. THE LITTLE GREEN CAP. Canvas. 51 × 30 cm. Washington, Freer Gallery of Art.

The model is Lily Pamington, who was one of the Soho children painted by the artist about 1896–1900.

112. LITTLE ROSE OF LYME REGIS. Canvas. 51·4 × 31·1 cm. Boston, Museum of Fine Arts.

Painted during the summer of 1895 while the artist was staying at the Red Lion Hotel at Lyme Regis, at the same time as *The Master Smith* (Boston). The artist's letters to his wife when she had returned to London leaving him there indicate that he had undergone an artistic crisis but that he had found his way. According to Pennell, *Life*, II, pp. 166–167, Whistler claimed that in these two pictures 'he really had solved the problem of carrying on his work as he wished to until it was finished and, technically, they are as accomplished as anything he ever did.' The picture seems to have been exhibited at the Boston Museum of Fine Arts in 1895 and was purchased by the Museum in 1896.

113. THE DUET. Lithograph. 24·5 × 16·2 cm. W. 64. 1894.

114. MRS. CHARLES WHIBLEY READING. Panel. 21·2 × 12·7 cm. Glasgow University, Birnie Philip Bequest.

Painted in 1894 in the drawing room of Whistler's house in Paris, 110 Rue du Bac.

115. PURPLE AND GOLD: PHRYNE THE SUPERB, BUILDER OF TEMPLES. Panel. 23·6×13·7 cm. Washington, Freer Gallery of Art.

Painted in 1898 and exhibited at the International Society in 1901 and the Paris Salon of 1902. The artist told the Pennells: 'would she be more superb – more truly the Builder of Temples – had I painted her what is called life-size by the foolish critics who always bring out their foot rule? Is it a question of feet and inches when you look at her?' (*Life*, II, p .206).

116. ROSE AND BROWN: LA CIGALE. Panel. 21·7× 12·6 cm. Washington, Freer Gallery of Art.

First exhibited at the International Society in 1899.

117. A SEATED GIRL HOLDING A BABY. Black crayon with flesh-coloured pastel on brown paper. Butterfly signature. 27·9×18·1 cm. Glasgow University, Birnie Philip Gift.

Exhibited in the late 1890's.

118. VENUS ASTARTE. Pastel on paper. 27·5×18·4 cm. Butterfly signature. Washington, Freer Gallery of Art.

One of the nude studies of the late 1890's.

119. GREY AND GOLD: THE GOLDEN BAY, IRELAND. Panel. 14×24 cm. Butterfly signature. Private Collection.

Whistler spent the summer of 1900 at a house called 'Craigie', at Sutton, six miles from Dublin 'on the spit of sand which connects the Hill of Howth with the mainland on the north side of Dublin Bay. This picture formerly belonged to R. A. Canfield, the gambler.

120. AJACCIO, CORSICA. 12·4×21·1 cm. Butterfly signature. Cambridge, Mass., Fogg Art Museum.

Whistler who fell ill in Marseilles on his return from North Africa was advised to cross over to Corsica. He stayed at the Hotel Schweizerhof in Ajaccio. He told Mrs. Pennell that the Curator of the museum there had offered him the use of a studio. 'The first day I was there, he watched me but said nothing until the afternoon. Then – "But, Mr. Whistler, I have looked at you, I have been watching. You are all nerves, you do nothing. You try to, but you cannot settle down to it. What you need is rest – to do nothing – not to try to do anything." All of a sudden, you know, it struck me that I had never rested, that I never had done this thing, that it was the one thing I needed! And I put myself down to doing nothing – amazing, you know. No more sketch-books – no more plates. I just sat in the sun and slept. I was cured. . . .' This was not strictly accurate, as while in Ajaccio he made a number of small oils, watercolours and etchings (*Life*, II, pp. 266–267).

121. ARRANGEMENT IN BLACK AND GOLD: COMTE ROBERT DE MONTESQUIOU. Canvas. 205·7×88·8 cm. Butterfly signature. New York, Frick Collection.

The sitter, who was a well-known dandy and a man of letters, sat to the artist seventeen times during a month's stay in London in 1891.
Edmond de Goncourt reported that 'the preliminary sketch, with Whistler, is apparently a mad rush at the canvas, one or two hours of feverish frenzy, from which the thing emerges all wrapped up in its covering. Then there are long, long sittings, during which most of the time the painter brings his brush up to the canvas, does not touch it, throws the brush away and takes another – with the result that in three hours he will add about fifty touches to the painting, each touch, in his words, removing one veil from the sketch's covering. Sittings in which it seemed to Montesquiou that Whistler with his fixed attention was emptying him for life, was "pumping away" something of his individuality.' (*Pages from the Goncourt Journal*, translated by Robert Baldick, 1962, p. 166.) Montesquiou also referred to the portrait in his Memoirs, 1923, pp. 260–2. He was on close terms with the artist, addressing to him a considerable number of letters which are now at Glasgow University. He gave Whistler in part payment of the Portrait the French Empire bedstead which had been presented to his ancestress by Napoleon I when she was governess of the young King of Rome. The picture was shown in the Salon of 1894. According to the Pennells, *Journal* (p. 270) the artist was furious when he heard in 1902 that Montesquiou had sold the portrait to Canfield.

122. PORTRAIT OF A. J. EDDY. Canvas. 210×93·3cm. Butterfly signature. Chicago, Art Institute.

Arthur Jerome Eddy (1859–1920) was a Chicago lawyer. He was a keen collector and sought out Whistler when he was little known in the United States and in 1893 commissioned him to paint his portrait. This was painted in Whistler's studio in the rue Notre des Champs, Paris in 1894. Eddy told him that the portrait had to be finished by a certain date and, although the artist was unaccustomed to accepting any time limit, he complied with the request. He told the Pennells (*Life*, II, p. 156) 'Well, you know, he is the only man who ever did get a picture out of me on time, while I worked and he waited.' It was finished by the stated time, but not sent to Chicago until the following year as Whistler kept on giving it finishing touches.

Eddy wrote a remarkable book on the artist, *Recollections and Impressions of James A. McNeill Whistler* in 1904. He also published a pioneering volume *Cubists and Post-Impressionists* in 1914.

123. PORTRAIT OF GEORGE W. VANDERBILT. Canvas. 206×94 cm. Washington, National Gallery of Art.

This portrait of the 'modern Philip' was started in Paris in 1897 but was never properly finished; however the sitter lent it to the Memorial Exhibition of 1905. The artist also painted Mrs. Vanderbilt – an oval picture entitled *Ivory and Gold*, which was sent to the Salon of 1902. Vanderbilt was a pallbearer at Whistler's funeral.

124. GOLD AND BROWN: SELF PORTRAIT. Canvas. 95·8×51·8 cm. Glasgow University, Birnie Philip Gift.

Already in being by May 1898 when Pennell saw it in Paris, the picture seems to have been partly repainted after having been shown at the American section of the Exposition Universelle of 1900.

125. PORTRAIT SKETCH OF A LADY. Canvas. 67·5×50 cm. Washington, Freer Gallery of Art.

This unfinished picture is in a frame apparently decorated by the artist. This once belonged to T. R. Way, the artist and the author of two books on Whistler.

126. PORTRAIT OF CHARLES L. FREER. Panel. 51·8×317 cm. Washington, Freer Gallery of Art.

Charles L. Freer, the founder of the Freer Gallery of Art, Washington, was a collector of Oriental art and modern American art. He bought many works from Whistler and became a firm friend; a number of letters by the artist to him are in the Gallery. The portrait was started in 1902 but only came into the sitter's possession after the artist's death.

127. DOROTHY SEATON: A DAUGHTER OF EVE. Canvas. 51·5×31·7 cm. Glasgow University, Birnie Philip Gift.

Painted in 1902 and exhibited at the Memorial Exhibition of 1905. She was an Irish model whose face reminded the artist of Hogarth's *Shrimp Girl* in the National Gallery, London.

128. GOLD AND BROWN: SELF PORTRAIT. Canvas. 64·77×47 cm. Butterfly signature. Washington, National Gallery of Art.

The artist wears the rosette of the Légion d'Honneur. Painted in about 1900 and formerly owned by George W. Vanderbilt.

129. DETAIL OF FRONTISPIECE.

THE PALACES, VENICE. Etching, 1880. K. 187.

LIST OF TEXT ILLUSTRATIONS

BIBLIOGRAPHICAL NOTE

As yet there is no oeuvre catalogue of Whistler's oil paintings, although one is being prepared by Mr. Andrew McLaren Young of Glasgow University. Whistler's etchings are illustrated in E. G. Kennedy's four volumes of 1910 and the lithographs in his publication of 1914. For catalogue details concerning his graphic work reference is necessary to Mansfield's book of 1909 (etchings) and T. R. Way's book of 1905 (lithographs).

A full bibliography of writings about Whistler published before 1910, which contains much of the relevant material, was issued in 1910. There is also a valuable annotated bibliography in the catalogue of the Whistler exhibition held at the Arts Council in 1960. Reference should also be made to the catalogue of the exhibition *Prélude à Whistler* held at the Centre Culturel Américain, Paris, in 1961. Much information about Whistler and his friends is to be found in the two volume life of him published by E. R. and J. Pennell in 1908 and their Whistler *Journal* of 1921. There is a good general book on Whistler by James Laver published in 1930 (2nd edition, revised, 1951) and a study of his art, *Nocturne. The Art of James McNeill Whistler* by Denys Sutton, 1963.

No attempt has been made in the notes on the plates to provide full catalogue details. I owe much to the notes in the Arts Council Catalogue of 1960.

Henry and Walter Greaves: DANCING PLATFORM, CREMORNE GARDENS, WITH A PORTRAIT OF WHISTLER. Private Collection

LIST OF COLLECTIONS

The Publishers wish to thank all private owners and public galleries for permission to reproduce works from their collections.

AMSTERDAM
Rijksmuseum: 74, fig. 21

ANDOVER, Mass.
Addison Gallery of American Art: 20

BALTIMORE
Walters Art Gallery: 88, 89

BIRMINGHAM
Barber Institute of Fine Arts: 40

BOSTON
Isabella Stewart Gardner Museum: 33, 77
Museum of Fine Arts: 22, 84, 112

CAMBRIDGE, Mass.
Fogg Art Museum: 48, 63, 78, 80, 86, 89, 90, 97, 120

CHICAGO
Art Institute: 45, 83, 122

CINCINNATI
Art Museum: 7

DETROIT
Institute of Arts: 59, 70

DUBLIN
E. Swift Newton: 2

FARMINGTON, Conn.
Hill-Stead Museum: 19

GLASGOW
City Art Gallery and Museum: 57
University, Birnie Philip Gift: 52, 96, 100, 109, 114, 117, 124, 127

HARTFORD, Conn.
Wadsworth Atheneum: 18

LONDON
Miss J. Alexander: 65
British Museum: Figs. 3, 13
National Gallery: Figs. 19, 22
Private Collection: 34
Tate Gallery: Frontispiece, 35, 41, 56, 64, 66, 67
Victoria and Albert Museum: Fig. 14
Julius H. Weitzner: Figs. 4, 5

MADRID
Prado: Fig. 18

MONTPELLIER
Musée Fabre: Fig. 1

NEW ORLEANS
Mr. and Mrs. Charles C. Henderson: 102

NEW YORK
Frick Collection: 36, 61, 71, 91, 121
Metropolitan Museum of Art: 68, 73, 76, 92
Mr. and Mrs. John Hay Whitney: 11

OXFORD
Ashmolean Museum: 75

PARIS
Louvre: 3, 53; figs. 10, 11, 12, 20

PHILADELPHIA
Museum of Art: 93; Fig. 2
John G. Johnson Collection: 28, 79

PITTSBURGH
Carnegie Institute: 95

PRIVATE COLLECTION: 38, 119, p. 199

ST. LOUIS, Mo.
City Art Museum: Fig. 9

SAN FRANCISCO
Mrs. A. B. Spreckels: Fig. 15

U.S.A. PRIVATE COLLECTION: 51

VIENNA
Oesterreichische Galerie: Fig. 26

WASHINGTON
Corcoran Gallery of Art: 21
Freer Gallery of Art: 1, 9, 13, 26, 30, 37, 39, 42, 43, 44, 49, 60, 62, 81, 82, 94, 101, 103, 104, 105, 106, 110, 111, 115, 116, 118, 125, 126
National Gallery of Art: 25, 27, 123, 128

WORCESTER, Mass.
Art Museum: 72